Urbanization in Developing Countries

Urbanization in Papua New Guinea:
A Study of Ambivalent Townsmen

Urbanization in Developing Countries

edited by Kenneth Little

V. F. Costello: *Urbanization in the Middle East*
Josef Gugler and William G. Flanagan: *Urbanization and Social Change in West Africa*
Hal B. Levine and Marlene Wolfzahn Levine: *Urbanization in Papua New Guinea: A Study of Ambivalent Townsmen*
Malcolm Cross: *Urbanization and Urban Growth in the Caribbean: An Essay on Social Change in Dependent Societies*

Urbanization in Papua New Guinea

A Study of Ambivalent Townsmen

HAL B. LEVINE

MARLENE WOLFZAHN LEVINE

CAMBRIDGE UNIVERSITY PRESS

Cambridge
London   New York   Melbourne

Published by the Syndics of the Cambridge University Press
The Pitt Building, Trumpington Street, Cambridge CB2 1RP
Bentley House, 200 Euston Road, London NW1 2DB
32 East 57th Street, New York, NY 10022, USA
296 Beaconsfield Parade, Middle Park, Melbourne 3206, Australia

© Cambridge University Press 1979

First published 1979

Printed in Great Britain by
Cox & Wyman Ltd, London, Fakenham and Reading

Library of Congress Cataloguing in Publication Data
Levine, Hal. B., 1947–
Urbanization in Papua New Guinea.
(Urbanization in developing countries).
Bibliography: p.
Includes index.
1. Urbanization – Papua New Guinea. 2. Rural–
urban migration – Papua New Guinea. 3. Sociology,
Urban. I. Levine, Marlene Wolfzahn, 1949–
joint author. II. Title.
HT149.P35L48   301.36′0995′3   78–58795
ISBN 0–521–22230–3 hard covers
ISBN 0–521–29410–X paperback

Contents

Acknowledgements

We would like to express our gratitude to Professor Paula Brown Glick of the State University of New York at Stony Brook. Without her help and inspiration we might never have gone to Papua New Guinea and would certainly have never written this book.

We would like to thank Professor Kenneth Little (the editor of this series), Dr Colin Day (our editor at Cambridge University Press) and the Press's reader for their helpful comments and criticisms. Dr Nancy Bowers of Auckland University read the first three chapters and reassured us with her positive response. Dr Ron May kindly supplied us with discussion papers from the Papua New Guinea Institute of Applied Social and Economic Research which proved very helpful in updating information on employment and migration. This book also benefited from a stimulation to do research and to share knowledge between disciplines fostered by the University of Papua New Guinea. Mrs Margaret Hewlett, Mrs Sandra Beath and Mrs P. Murray of Victoria University of Wellington typed the manuscript with unfailing good will and good cheer.

Finally, our very special thanks to our respective parents for their early and continuing encouragement and support.

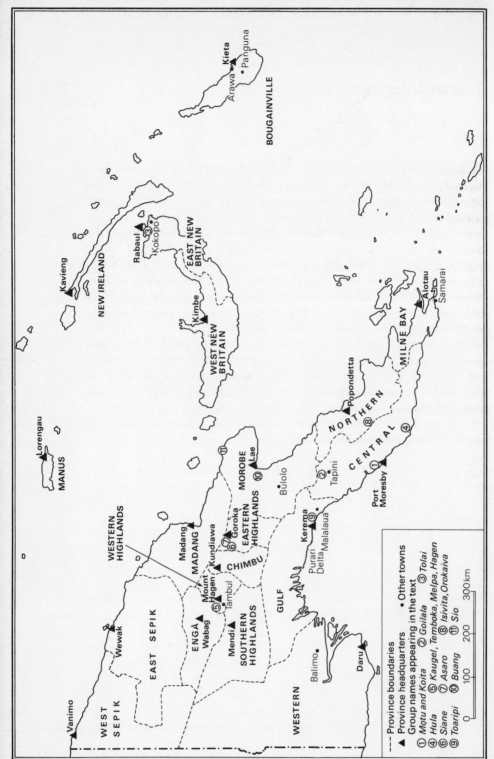

Papua New Guinea

1. Introduction

We lived in Papua New Guinea for two and a half years, mostly in Port Moresby and Mount Hagen, but also visited many other urban centres, and in that time we rarely heard Papua New Guineans say a kind word about their towns. They complained of how expensive it was to live in the towns, and of the violence there, and of the danger and difficulties involved in living amid so many strangers. But even though they would denigrate town life, the migrants seemed to crave the excitement and exotic quality of what was still a largely European colonial environment. They enjoyed the night-life and sophistication, the money (when it came in) and the escape from village responsibilities, and they appreciated the chance to learn and experience new things.

At the same time, however, people seemed to perceive these as being wrong or even decadent reasons for leaving one's home. The message from most townsmen we met was pretty clear, that a person's proper place was back in the village. The fact that one was addicted to town life was nothing to be proud of.

This ambivalence towards city life was like an undercurrent in Papua New Guinea. It typically surfaced when people were feeling frustrated, unhappy or nostalgic for some reason, or when they were under direct pressure from kinfolk in their village. Then they often talked of going home and would sometimes leave quite suddenly, vowing not to return. But when people did go back they would boast about their urban experiences and, despite promises to the contrary made to their families and to themselves, they would probably turn up in Port Moresby or Lae again, laughing about how boring and uncomfortable village life can be. One's home was in the village, but there was a new life in the towns.

The towns of Papua New Guinea were originally colonial centres, always planned by and for white men, and thus essentially alien places. Colonization and extensive contact were relatively recent, and independence came only in 1975, making this one of the newest of 'developing nations'. As in the rest of the Third World, and despite their late start, substantial numbers of Papua New Guineans are moving into their urban areas. But rural life is still vigorous in the nation as a whole, and people are not very likely to be forced into town by the desperate rural poverty or severe land pressure one finds in parts of Asia, Latin America and even the Pacific. There is a real, viable rural alternative for Papua New

Guinean townsmen. Traditional culture and social organization are very much alive and are even having a significant impact on the towns themselves as the people gradually change them from alien places into urban centres uniquely their own. The course of Papua New Guineans' adjustment to town life and the modification of their urban environment through the use of Papua New Guinean social idioms provides the theme of this monograph.

We have tried to synthesize the research that has been done in urban Papua New Guinea and to produce a meaningful and coherent picture of the main trends of urbanization as a social process. In order to accomplish this, it has been necessary to integrate the information by means of a conceptual scheme which is capable of pulling disparate studies together, but also flexible enough to accommodate the range of data and perspectives used by various researchers. The approach we have taken directs attention to the interaction between people and their urban environments and allows for an appreciation of the Papua New Guinean response to a type of social change that is occurring in most developing nations.

Analytical framework

Urbanization is viewed in various ways by social scientists. Perspectives differ not only by discipline but within the same subject as well. Rather than engage in an extended discussion of the various meanings and theoretical perspectives used in studies of urbanization in the Third World[1] we will concentrate on a presentation of our own views (developed from the overall literature, local case-studies and our own fieldwork) which provide the theoretical framework for this book's organization.

Discussing urbanization as a social process implies a focus on 'elements of culture, behaviour patterns and ideas' that are characteristic of towns (Little 1974: 7). Although some scholars concentrate on urbanization as involving a distinctive way of life (Wirth 1938) and one which greatly differs from that of rural villages, everyone who has done urban research in Papua New Guinea has recognized that elements of rural behaviour, culture and ideas greatly affect urban social organization. The distinction between rural and urban social behaviour may be quite subtle. In later chapters we will show how rural idioms of behaviour may produce distinctive social forms in urban environments. It would be easy to miss the

---

[1] General summaries and critiques of anthropological and sociological approaches to urbanization in the Third World may be found in Mitchell (1966) and Gutkind (1974) who refer readers to the numerous other sources available. Hanna and Hanna (1971) give a concise discussion of various viewpoints from different social sciences and Breese (1966) also discusses some of the different meanings of urbanization.

importance of these idioms, however, if we used a framework which reified the urban sphere by treating it as a self-contained social system.[2]

It is crucial to avoid this tendency. In countries such as Papua New Guinea, where urbanization is such a recent phenomenon that the majority of urban dwellers were born in 'tribal' villages, it is more useful to conceive of our task as an analysis of the adaptation of urban immigrants to what is for them a new type of social environment.

Although that environment does differ in important ways from the rural one, the notion of adaptation allows us to view urban immigrants as bringing behaviour patterns into town with them, abandoning, modifying and retaining them as they are exposed to various social situations. Some of these situations may be best dealt with by the use of rurally developed social idioms while others may call for responses in terms of more peculiarly urban behaviour.

Towns are usually conceived of as having a number of distinguishing characteristics. Hanna and Hanna (1971: 6), for example, in their study of urbanization in black Africa, have identified relatively dense populations, a large number of social roles and a relative permanence of population and socio-economic infrastructure as being 'criteria of towns'. Geographers and demographers often specify a certain minimum population as an additional criterion of urbanism. Relatively little attention has been paid to the problem of what constitutes an urban centre in Papua New Guinea. The local Bureau of Statistics classifies settlements with a minimum population of 500, population density of 500 per square mile (approximately 200 per square kilometre), and a 'generally urban character', as towns for census purposes. This definition might seem excessively liberal to many social scientists, but even centres small enough to fit such a minimal definition may be towns in the local context. However, even though we feel the Bureau of Statistics definition is a defensible one, the fact that no substantial body of research data exists for towns with populations of less than 10,000 perhaps makes this a moot point.

In any case, we follow Gulick here. He stresses that size of population is less important to a sociological definition of 'urban' than the sort of traits mentioned by the Hannas (Gulick 1974). In Papua New Guinea all of these are associated with the presence of significant concentrations of non-indigenous people and the economic and social institutions created by them. An expatriate presence, along with the other criteria mentioned, defines a particular area as urban in Papua New Guinea.

When rural tribesmen or peasants move from their village to an environment with urban characteristics they typically become involved in

[2] Discussions of how to conceptualize the urban system abound in the urban anthropological literature. The sources mentioned in the previous footnote will introduce and refer the student to most of these.

social situations that result in increased interactive range, in other words, situations in which they must deal with people who have either no place, or an uncertain one, in their particular rural system of social relations. Entering a position in a complex division of labour often involve the urbanite in a greater differentiation of roles and density of role relationships than in rural areas.

Some anthropologists have suggested that urbanization may profitably be approached in terms of an analysis of the roles assumed by townsmen: their combination, differentiation and availability. The urban social field may be conceived of as allowing for considerable flexibility of roles and role relationships in some spheres of urban life while prescribing particular combinations of roles in others (Banton 1973 and Southall 1973b, cited in Rew 1974: 214).

Viewing urban environments in a similar way we may conceptually distinguish two aspects of urban life which present themselves to formerly rural tribesmen settling in towns, demanding their entry into conceptually separate but interrelated fields of social relationships. Aspects of city life which relate to personal security, and leave an individual more or less free to choose his own associates, may be approached by the establishment of different sorts of social relationships than those which are entered into as a result of going about the more structured tasks of working for wages, living in multi-ethnic housing areas, dealing with bureaucracies, the foreign domination of business and supervisory positions, etc.

Like most newly developing nations, Papua New Guinea is not a comprehensive welfare state. High unemployment, housing shortages and the presence of known tribal enemies and potentially dangerous strangers are factors which necessitate a degree of mutuality on the part of migrants. People from rural areas may also need considerable urban socialization to cope with the mechanics of transport, job-hunting, the use of other urban facilities, etc. The strangeness of the environment also has the potential to produce loneliness and alienation if congenial and familiar company is not found. These exigencies of urban life may be most successfully met by the establishment of social relationships with people on whom the migrant has some moral claim, for example, a kinsman or fellow ethnic. The social networks constructed in the course of establishing personal bases in the urban environment may then be built in terms of behavioural styles and idioms that show great continuity with those used in rural areas. Although these strategies of establishing social relationships may have rural referents and idioms, their use in an urban environment is bound to produce social forms which are in some ways distinctly urban. But it is in this sphere, relating to personal security and establishing oneself in town, that roles and role relationships are left open or flexible by the urban system and the migrant most free to use his own personal and cultural styles.

Having such bases of security allows new townsmen to partake of the wider urban social field and weather the crises (most notably unemployment) which may overtake them in it. But behaviour and social relationships on the job, in relation to neighbours, government officials, expatriates, etc., are likely to be phrased in ways that are less continuous with rural social idioms. In contrast to the close relationships one has with kinsmen and fellow ethnics, those in the wider social sphere are likely to be more transitory, segmental, and superficial, though of course friends may be made here as well. Such relationships may be phrased in terms of specific work and racial roles, more general socio-economic statuses, etc. – idioms which are more or less peculiar to the urban environment.

We are then suggesting an approach to urbanization in countries like Papua New Guinea in terms of examining sets of social relationships, some of which allow townsmen to use rural strategies to adapt to urban life while others demand more urban and western behavioural patterns and idioms. Of course, these sets are unlikely to be as readily separable on the level of everyday life as they may be as sociological abstractions (or 'ideal types') which help provide a framework for analysis. For a better understanding of urban reality as reflected in day-to-day experiences we should recognize that the two sets of social relationships discussed above are necessarily linked and interwoven. It would be a gross oversimplification to ignore this linkage. To do so would imply a false dichotomy of 'native' aspects of urbanization on the one hand and purely introduced ones on the other. The really interesting social action is in our opinion the creation of new kinds of urban systems, out of what often were formerly alien colonial administrative centres, through the social action of townsmen who (in the case of Papua New Guinea) were excluded from those centres in the past except as temporary menial workers.

This creation may come about substantially through the selective exchange of idioms between the spheres. If townsmen attempt to establish close personal ties in the work situation, for example, by extending rural idioms to it, the idioms and the work situation may be subtly altered and take on a new flavour. On the other hand, socio-economic status differences from the more western urban sphere may take on significance in relations between kin and fellow ethnics, significantly altering a mode of relationship with important rural referents. By concentrating our synthesis on the interrelating of these conceptually separable spheres of social relationships, we feel we will be able to develop an understanding of urbanization as a social process in Papua New Guinea.

In summary, we will view townsmen as influencing urban systems while being influenced by them. In order to grasp the way in which this is occurring, we need to understand how social action is initiated within the context of certain constraints and incentives to behaviour which are imposed by the urban environment and the migrants' status and background. We should try to understand how social action is formulated (Berger and Luckmann 1966, Blumer 1969), how situations are seen by townsmen and the way in which new joint action (developing as a result of urbanization) emerges out of a framework of previous patterns of behaviour and requisites of the urban system, which is itself fundamentally affected by this dynamic social process. This to us is the essence of urbanization as a social process.

Organization of the monograph

Papua New Guinea's towns developed in the context of a colonial encounter which affected the development of particular urban centres and the urbanization process. In the second chapter we consider the main elements of the colonial situation, the policies and practices of various administrations, and the general nature of indigenous societies and their response to colonialism, as they bear on urban development. The overall lack of industrialization, late development of facilities for permanent indigenous residents, urban morphology, etc., are all important aspects of urbanism which are direct results of the colonial situation.

Chapter Three is concerned with the peopling of the towns. Migration itself is, of course, significantly affected by colonial policy and labour needs. But as we shall see, rural–urban movement has become increasingly detached from formal controls. The kinds of people who do come to town, their areas of origin, skills, reasons for coming, perception of the advantages of living in towns, commitment to an urban or rural future, position in the emerging socio-economic hierarchy, greatly affect urban life-styles and are the main topics discussed in this chapter.

With the background provided by the second and third chapters, we move our discussion towards urban social relationships. Chapter Four examines the establishment of primary relationships in urban areas through the use of kinship, ethnicity, traditional and urban transactional styles and idioms. The use of such primary relationships and principles of categorization to establish a base in the towns, their effect on the composition of neighbourhoods, leadership, women's roles, and the importance of strategies aimed at the maintenance of rural ties, are all part of the continuing process of maintaining a secure urban niche.

The fifth chapter is concerned with the application of some of these same idioms to what we have called the wider social field. It examines the world of work, the relationship between job prestige and individual prestige, the importance of socio-economic categories, inter-ethnic interaction patterns, and élites. The tendency of townsmen to perceive, categorize and stereotype each other in pervasively ethnic terms is also discussed in detail.

Although we maintain that Papua New Guineans have been creating a new urban culture, Chapter Six focuses on an aspect of urbanism which has been less amenable to penetration by local social idiom. Melanesians have found that dealing with bureaucratic organizations is a major stumbling block in coping with town life. This is demonstrated in a discussion of urban government, voluntary associations, businessmen and bureaucracy. Colonial-style urban institutions and local people will have to adapt mutually to each other's presence for the emergence of truly national urban centres to eventuate.

Chapter Seven begins with a critique of various views of local urbanization. This is followed by a comparative discussion of towns in other parts of the world which is designed to point out the relatively unique as well as the more generally shared aspects of the Papua New Guinean situation. We then summarize our account of the towns as Papua New Guinean places and conclude with an overview of problems and prospects for the future.

2. Urban development and form

Our aim in this chapter is to sketch the overall development and form of urban areas in Papua New Guinea in light of the country's colonial history. We stress general trends in order to show how policies and perceptions about natives, and their own late familiarity with towns and westernization, have combined to cast urban forms in a particular mould. After a consideration of aspects of traditional societies, and various sections dealing with colonial developments, housing policy is stressed as an especially visible and important instance of the effect of colonial policy on urban morphology and social differentiation. The chapter ends with a discussion of urban variety to balance the emphasis on general trends.

The relevance of traditional societies to opening a discussion of early urban developments may not be immediately apparent, especially since we pointed out in the introduction to this monograph that Papua New Guinea's towns were founded by expatriates. Unlike many other areas of the developing world such as Latin America, Asia, the Middle East and West Africa (but in common with the rest of the island South Pacific), there were no indigenous pre-colonial urban settlements in New Guinea. As we will show in some detail below, native people were given little scope to participate actively in the development of their country's towns except as hewers of wood and drawers of water until late in the colonial period. Nevertheless, even from the beginning, the nature of local societies and cultures themselves acted as a crucial influence on the development of the formerly colonial centres.

We should point out, however, that any attempt at a brief overview of Papua New Guinea's traditional societies is bound to be problematic. There are two apparently contradictory avenues of approach to take. One would be to stress that in an area of 12,000 essentially independent villages, whose people speak approximately 700 different languages and have been the subject of more intensive anthropological research than any comparable region of the world, a capsule overview is really impossible. While we could perhaps bypass the issue entirely and simply refer the reader to the available literature, this would prevent us from showing that certain aspects of the overall socio-cultural landscape of Papua New Guinea fundamentally influenced the urbanization process.

The second path (which we have taken) is paradoxically to stress that local societies are very similar indeed – at least with respect to their degree of overall socio-cultural integration. We will, then, be referring more to a common level of structural complexity than to aspects of socio-cultural diversity. As much as we feel that students of Melanesian society should not be mesmerized by the area's uniformity of societal scale or its great cultural diversity (Barth 1971), we would argue that this very general approach is most advisable here. Although each particular local culture or social structure may influence urbanization in a variety of ways, the available urban literature is by no means extensive enough for us to compare each group's experiences and impact nor to arrive at a complete understanding of all the comparative implications of cultural difference for urbanization. Although we do attempt this for a limited number of groups and circumstances later in the book, what we wish to stress in this chapter is that the interaction of a certain type of society and variety of colonialism has greatly influenced urban development in Papua New Guinea. Hence the discussion which follows presents only a basic overview of a situation which may, if urban ethnographies become extensive and detailed enough, eventually warrant more detailed comparative ethnographic analysis.

Traditional societies[1]

Papua New Guinea's indigenous settlement patterns and social organization reflect the fragmented nature of the island's environment, its isolation from the eastern and western centres of civilization, and the needs of small-scale subsistence economies. Administrative policy was greatly influenced by the distribution and lack of political and economic centralization of the country's relatively small population (approximately 2.5 million people) which was spread out over 700,000 square kilometres. Papua New Guineans' responses to urbanization are, of course, importantly related to the type of societies they come from, as well as the roles colonial administrators allowed native people to play in urban life.

Local indigenous societies are typified by a lack of elaborate social hierarchies. Acknowledged leaders are men of influence who (in the great majority of societies) have achieved positions which rest on a base of personal qualities and relationships. 'Big-men' create obligations and followers by bringing prestige or material benefit to others through their

---

[1] The literature dealing with local traditional societies is enormous. The three-volume *Ethnographic Bibliography of New Guinea* provides sources prior to 1968. The *Encyclopedia of Papua New Guinea* provides summary articles on various aspects of societal scale such as economics, politics, etc. An overview of Melanesian settlement patterns, location and trade is found in Brookfield with Hart (1971). Bulmer (1975) provides an up-to-date summary account of the area's pre-history.

astute management of generally available resources. They neither occupy a position in a formal government bureaucracy nor control exclusive title to resources. Access to land (the primary means of production) is regulated by the kinship system, and all members of a kin group have land rights. Bureaucracies, police forces and social stratification (other than on a basis of sex and age) are aspects of life introduced by outsiders which assume greatest importance in towns. Traditional social systems were organized in terms of kinship idioms, not caste or class.

Such personal forms of leadership and social organization, resting on obligation and support by local kin, are effective in small-scale societies. Traditional societies were indeed small, rarely extending past local settlements of a few hundred people. Although tribes in the highlands, for example, may have up to 8000 members, these are ephemeral entities, often split by fighting, which rarely function as units.

In marked contrast to the world economy which is making ever greater inroads into Papua New Guinea, traditional economic activities are subsistence-oriented and do not involve elaborate division of labour nor full-time specialization of tasks, except on the basis of age and sex. The main subsistence activity is vegetable gardening, which provides for the bulk of the diet, and (on the coast) fishing. Aside from pigs and dogs there were no domesticated animals. Although pigs are crucial exchange resources and Papua New Guineans seem as attached to them as certain Africans are to cattle, they compete with humans for food, cannot be herded and do not provide milk. There was no transhumescence in Papua New Guinea. Everyone was in some way dependent on the production of vegetables from small plots worked with simple tools. Although the anthropological literature details the existence of various forms of shell money, the production of highly sophisticated works of art, and a series of long-range trade systems (e.g. the Kula described by Malinowski (1922)), these operated within the context of the political situation outlined above and the great predominance of subsistence activities in the economy.

Although Papua New Guinean societies are homogeneous in terms of their scale (or level of structural complexity) this is only a very general aspect of social systems. A major theme in the extensive anthropological literature on Papua New Guinea's traditional societies is the extraordinary cultural diversity, mentioned above, which coexists with this unity of scale. This diversity itself is a fact of great moment to Papua New Guinea as a nation state, because it is in the towns that people become most aware of this heterogeneity and act on it in interesting ways.

The island of New Guinea was peopled by many different waves of pre-historic migrants. The history of these migrations is largely unknown, and may never be fully understood because of the length of time over which they occurred and the great number of movements and local developments which must have happened to produce such a physically and culturally diverse population. The complex natural environment with its multitudinous ecological niches presented numerous possibilities for diverse socio-cultural adaptation. The broken terrain, extremely mountainous interior, scattered islands off the coast, and great areas of swamp, further served to fragment the population. If, as is suspected, people have been slowly drifting into such an environment for the past 50,000 years, it is not difficult to see how numerous and heterogeneous such small-scale societies could come to be. We can get some idea of the extent of this cultural diversity from the aforementioned fact that over 700 separate languages have been recorded in the country, many of which are seemingly unrelated to others.

The general picture presented by the country's traditional societies is, then, one of many social units scattered over a wide area. Broken terrain, a largely unknown but certainly complex history of migration to the island, and the existence of a variety of physical types and cultures, create a great diversity of societies, which, despite their other differences, share a unity of overall societal scale.

The colonizers

As was mentioned previously, this situation remained relatively undisturbed by outside pressures until the nineteenth century. In 1828 the Dutch claimed part of New Guinea, setting the future of the western half of the island apart from that of the eastern side. Irian Jaya, formerly Dutch New Guinea, is now a province of Indonesia. The eastern half of the large island, now called Papua New Guinea, was itself divided between two colonial powers until World War I.

Eastern New Guinea was not colonized until the 1880s. In 1884, the British established a protectorate over south-eastern New Guinea, and were followed a few days later by the Germans who began hoisting their flag at various points along the north-east coast. By 1885, the Germans and the British had defined the boundaries of their respective claims, dividing the eastern half of New Guinea between them (Biksup, Jinks and Nelson 1968).

In 1901 the British Colonial Office transferred its claims to Australia (at whose insistence it had established the protectorate in the first place). In 1905 British New Guinea was officially declared to be an Australian territory and was renamed Papua.

The German government initially permitted their colony to be governed by the Neu Guinea Kompagnie which was mainly interested in securing an economic return from the territory and attracting settlers. The Kompagnie's business and settlement plans largely failed, however, and the Imperial government took over administration from 1899. During World War I, a small Australian expeditionary force ousted the Germans. As a result of this action Australia was given a League of Nations mandate over the north, which became the Mandated Territory of New Guinea. Since Papua was an Australian territory, and New Guinea a mandated one, separate administrations (which pursued notably different policies) were maintained by the Australians. It was not until after World War II that Papua and New Guinea were administratively united and the colonial framework for an independent Papua New Guinea established (ibid.).

Reasons for colonization

The colonial powers' approach to colonization greatly affected the growth of towns. As was mentioned, the Germans looked upon New Guinea as a possible economic asset, but their hopes for profit and settlement never materialized. One important reason for this was that New Guinea quickly got a well-deserved reputation for being unhealthy. Many of those foreigners who did come to the country died of malaria. In addition, labourers and supplies proved difficult to obtain and Australia and New Zealand were probably much more attractive South Pacific countries in which to settle. Despite the overall lack of settlement, much of the Gazelle Peninsula in East New Britain (a particularly lush and fertile area) was taken over by European planters, as was land near Madang. Both proved to be trouble-spots for colonial authorities. When Australia took over in the north, land already in German hands was given to Australians. The mandated territory's administration was in future to be considerably influenced by expatriate demands for labour and commercial development (Biksup *et al.* 1968, Mair 1970, Rowley 1958, Sack 1973).

Britain was prodded into action in the south by Australian fears of a foreign presence in New Guinea. The Torres Straits, which separate Queensland from Papua New Guinea, are a vital shipping lane to Europe and the erstwhile British colonies in Australia were quite anxious for the Crown to claim the south coast. Having done so, the Colonial Office hastened to turn British New Guinea over to Australia, itself a developing nation unwilling to divert substantial resources to its new territory. Aside from where they had established mission stations (prior to the official declaration of the protectorate), there were few expatriates in Papua. In fact, by 1921 there were only 1300 European residents in each colony.

Papua remained a backwater territory whose administration acquired a reputation for opposition to white settlement (Joyce 1971). New Guinea, also relatively undeveloped, nonetheless had more invested in it than Papua, with more plantations, a better road system and more ports, which later became towns. This divergent development is an important political issue in present-day Papua New Guinea. Movements which aim to correct the imbalance have developed in Port Moresby and have greatly affected ethnic alignments throughout the country.

Both areas remained rather marginal colonies, however. There were no great mineral strikes, although miners opened significant tracts of territory searching for gold. Coconuts and rubber became the most consistent exports. After the German period little further land was alienated from natives and very few settlers arrived. Most expatriates worked for the missions and government, and never made up more than 1.5 per cent of the total population of either territory. In such circumstances there was no significant industrialization, and labour needs for the plantation industry were relatively light. Except for an early period of 'black-birding' (kidnapping Melanesians to work in Queensland sugar fields), early migration was slight and produced little dislocation. For most Papua New Guineans, the pre-World War II period of colonization meant little more than an occasional visit by a young European patrol officer who made people line up for census-taking and insisted that they dig latrines. Missionaries, initially confined to the coast, were perhaps the greatest agents of social change in rural areas during this period.

The extension of control and early growth of towns

A general lack of finance and staff, the rough terrain, small isolated nature of indigenous groups, lack of chiefs who could influence large numbers of followers, great diversity of local languages and a reluctance to make reprisals after attacks by indigenes, prevented the quick opening and effective colonial control of much of the interior. As a mechanism for the gradual integration of British New Guinea, a policy of dividing the country into districts was put into effect which became a model for future Australian administrations in both territories. Each administrative district was assigned a headquarters and resident magistrate whose duty it was to dispatch patrols throughout the area to investigate disturbances, hold trials, take census and ensure that government edicts affecting villages were obeyed. As areas were penetrated and patrolled, new districts and district headquarters were gazetted and these were further divided into sub-districts (Joyce 1971). District and sub-district headquarters became centres of whatever government facilities existed in any particular area, as well as foci of increasing European (and later, 'foreign native') population as staff was added to a district. Since both Europeans and Papua New Guineans living on or near government stations had cash but little choice of where to spend it, shops and markets for both western goods and local foodstuffs grew up in these areas which gradually became the country's towns. Since water transport was most feasible in the early colonial days, the first centres were small ports. Later, when aeroplanes were used to open the interior, district centres were sited around suitable airstrips (Brookfield with Hart 1971).

The Germans followed a similar procedure for establishing control of New Guinea. Despite the fact that their administration was short-lived, and patrols were mainly confined to areas near coastal plantations or parts of the interior deemed suitable for labour recruitment, a number of German stations became sites of future towns.

It was assumed by administrators that such posts would increase Papua New Guineans' familiarity with government aims through the patrols carried out from them and the introduction of European trade goods. An increase in influence would be apparent from a decrease in tribal fighting and an increase in the use of courts. Each post would be like a spot of oil which gradually spread over an absorbent surface. If enough spots were dropped, whole areas of control would emerge and eventually the entire country would be effectively colonized (West 1968: 162–3).

This pattern of opening up and splitting districts and sub-districts not only became a charter for the future pattern of urban growth, but substantially influenced the content and expression of urban social relationships. Not only could reference to one's own ethnic identity, or that of others whose traditional identities were unknown, be given in terms of patrol post or district headquarter names (which are usually more inclusive than indigenous socio-cultural units), but the name of the division itself would carry connotations of relative sophistication or primitiveness. Certain regions were opened in advance of others (e.g. coastal parts were opened well before the highlands which were not controlled until the 1950s). People from areas more accessible to colonial centres benefited in terms of earlier opportunities for education, with the result that they are now significantly over-represented in Papua New Guinea's universities and public service.

Ethnic stereotypes based on dichotomies of 'primitive' and 'civilized', a classificatory system of ethnic identity based on district of origin, basic inequalities of regional development which become important political issues, and the siting and growth of urban centres, are all directly attributable to those aspects of the colonial situation summarized above. Despite the production of some tensions, however, Papua New Guinea has fared relatively well at the hands of imperial powers. Indigenous social and cultural life was far from shattered and most Papua New Guineans largely escaped the brutality experienced by the native peoples of many other colonies (see, for example, West (1956)).

Aspects of urban growth

As one could expect in such marginal colonial territories, towns developed slowly. Established by and for colonial agents, they initially were small European outposts with a sprinkling of native servants, who usually lived in surrounding villages or barracks outside municipal boundaries. The growth of Port Moresby (discussed in Levine 1976, Oram 1976, Rew 1974, Ryan 1970, Stuart 1970 and Surmon 1971) is generally representative of trends in the rest of Papua New Guinea.[2]

Moresby, like other coastal towns, was established at the site of a deep-water anchorage. The advantages of its particular location on the Papuan coast were nearness to the telegraph station at Cookstown, Queensland, and the fact that the area is relatively sparsely populated, but by a group with extensive contacts up and down the south coast. As was the case in other parts of this reluctantly claimed colony, missionaries had been residing locally prior to adminstrators. Since the autochthonous people were then already somewhat familiar with Europeans it was relatively easy for colonial officials to establish themselves.

Port Moresby in the period from 1889 to 1941 has been aptly characterized as 'a small sleepy colonial backwater functioning mainly as an administrative centre. It was an Australian town from which Papuans were excluded except as workers' (Oram 1976: 51). Badili, then outside the town boundary, was the first significant housing area for indigenes aside from native villages. Local people were not permitted to live inside the town itself unless they inhabited servant quarters provided behind their employers' homes. Although people from local villages were relatively free to enter into wage employment, those from outside the immediate hinterland wishing to work in the town were bound to contract for a specified period after which they were sent home. The indigenous urban population prior to World War II was minimal. Moresby, today the largest town in the country, contained well under 1000 Papuans before 1942. The vast majority were single male manual workers whose lives in town were strictly curtailed by legislation relating to where they could live, when they were permitted out of doors, the facilities they were not allowed to use (i.e. certain swimming pools, beaches, shops, etc., frequented by whites), and even the clothing they could wear.

The overall impression one gets of pre-war urban areas is that they

---

[2] Summaries of the growth of all urban areas are provided in Jackson (1976a), and an overview of Melanesian urban development is given in Brookfield with Hart (1971). The histories of the following towns have also been described: Goroka (Munster 1973), Lae (Lucas 1972, Willis 1974), Mount Hagen (Levine 1976) and Rabaul (Epstein 1969).

were not places for natives. A few indigenous people were allowed in
them, mainly as servants or manual workers, but they were restricted as
much as possible in what was essentially a European social environment.
Papua New Guineans were given little scope for contributing anything to
urban social life, while the towns themselves have been aptly described as
'toeholds of an alien society' and 'bases for alien control' (Brookfield with
Hart 1971: 390).

With negligible industrialization, little rural development and minimal
urban migration, relatively few Papua New Guineans were more than
marginal participants in the cash economy. The war, however, served to
involve many men more deeply with the outside world as they were
recruited to serve as carriers or in other ways pressed to contribute to the
allied war effort. When the hostilities ended, these men had seen the
towns, worked with whites (often in closer circumstances than possible
before the war) and developed a desire for cash and manufactured
consumer goods that could not be met in the country's villages. These
developments coincided with a need for men to rebuild the colony's
centres which were all but destroyed during the hostilities.

Post-war towns were not merely built to pre-war standards. A great
increase in the scale of administration activity, expenditure and employment, together with improvements in transportation and a gradual lifting
of restraints on the movement of Melanesians, combined to transform
the nature of urban areas. These changes, primarily a consequence of
administrative expansion, were set in train by Australia's amalgamation
of the two territories and her realization that preparations for local
development and eventual self-government were necessary. Urban
populations increased directly with government expenditure. In the area
of education, for example, Papua New Guinea has gone in twenty-five
years from a country where schooling was almost wholly in mission
hands to a nation that has government primary and high schools in all
districts, two universities, a medical school, dental college, teachers'
colleges and a number of technical training institutions. Thousands
of expatriates have been brought in to work in this field alone and many
Papua New Guinean students have come from rural areas. Such increases
in urban populations attract services of various kinds and lately several
small industries have sprung up to provide goods for the growing urban
market.

Although this general pattern of growth makes the nation's towns fairly
homogeneous in some ways, their differing geographical areas, local
populations, links with other centres, particular colonial experiences and
developing industries provides a basis for urban diversity. The building of
the Highland Highway, which connects Lae with the coffee- and tea-
growing highlands, for example, has stimulated local development to the

point where Lae now challenges Port Moresby as a business centre. The link with the coast has facilitated a great expansion of highland centres (Goroka, Kundiawa, Mount Hagen and Mendi), helping to create towns out of patrol posts in little more than fifteen years. For these towns, as well as those recently built for south Bougainville's copper industry, future urban expansion may be less tied to government expenditure than in the past.

The urban landscape

Despite the sudden transition brought about by the war, expansion of administration spending and growth of urban populations, the colonial nature of Papua New Guinea's towns persisted and still continued to affect urban life. Although discriminatory legislation was gradually repealed (Stuart 1970), attitudes towards the role of indigenes in urban life and the provision of facilities for them were not matters easily changed by legislation. Even the administration which was liberalizing the law seemed to ignore the role of Papua New Guineans in urban development (Oram 1976). Native people were not, for example, included in urban census figures until 1966. The gradual provision of housing, the most fundamental of urban amenities, demonstrates how slow was the authorities' acceptance of Papua New Guineans as legitimate townsmen (Oram 1970, 1976; Surmon 1971).

In addition to mirroring government attitudes towards indigenous residence in towns, housing policy and the responses to it created a most concrete expression of urban form (Surmon 1971), both socially and spatially. The type of dwelling one inhabits is an important reflection of socio-economic status in the urban environment and a crucial resource as well.

As was mentioned above, the first urban migrants either lived in domestic quarters, or local villages and barracks outside municipal boundaries. After the war they were housed in old army barracks or other makeshift accommodation. Conditions in these were only suitable for single male workers; wives and children could only be housed in villages or self-made dwellings. This lack of suitable government, employer-provided, or low-cost private housing schemes for families has meant that a substantial portion of the urban population has had to build their own quarters. For a number of reasons, such as lack of space, a desire to live rent-free or with relations or friends of one's own choosing, interpersonal strife, etc., many single men also wish to build their own houses. These single and family dwellings became focal points for the growth of many 'squatter' or migrant settlements. One difficulty with this kind of self-help housing is that migrants have no land rights in urban areas. One way of short-circuiting this problem is to live over the water or on boats which can be anchored near amenities like markets. Although some canoe settlements exist (especially in Port Moresby), most people prefer to live on dry land and have some sort of food garden. In some towns (again, especially Port Moresby) which were points in indigenous long-distance trade networks, traditional ties can be exploited by migrants to gain housing sites in town. Gulf district people arriving in Port Moresby asked for land-use rights from the autochthonous Motu on the basis of old trading partnerships, and built homes on indigenously owned land within the capital's central area. These people can hardly be labelled squatters as they have obtained their land with the owners' permission.

Difficulties arise even in such initially friendly circumstances, however. A Motu landholder may be quite willing to allow a specific Gulf migrant to use his land, or even enter into a landlord–tenant relationship with a Highlander or other person to whom no traditional tie exists. But migrants' homes quickly become centres for other migrants related to the householder. Newcomers often wish to live near their relatives and usually have no other housing possibilities than to stay with them initially. Soon new houses go up near the first one and it is the initial migrant, not the landowner, who is consulted for permission to use a site. Eventually a settlement is formed as chain migration and the use of kinship ties creates a dense housing cluster which begins to take on characteristics of an ethnic neighbourhood. The friendly ties to the landowner may become less cordial as he tries to stop the growth of the settlement or get more rent out of the migrants who tend to view the area as theirs despite a lack of legal rights. The realization that they may someday be forced to leave inhibits many migrants from upgrading their houses. The government has tended until recently to ignore these problems either by denying the existence of the settlements on an official level or by refusing to get involved in native jurisdictional disputes. At the same time, the settlements allowed workers to establish themselves in towns at their own expense, saving both government and private employers significant amounts of money. The case of a Goilala migrant to Port Moresby, one of our earliest contacts there, illustrates how the development of such a settlement presented difficulties for native right-holders, migrants and government officials as well.

Our informant came to town in 1967, and moved into an overcrowded domestic servant's hut occupied by his brother-in-law. One day while riding on a bus he chanced to sit next to a senior lineage head of a nearby village. The two men struck up a conversation, sharing a flask of whisky which the Goilala happened to be carrying. They became quite friendly and our informant invited his companion back to his house. When the local man saw how miserable and cramped the Goilala's quarters were he offered to let him build a home on his own clan's land. The offer was eagerly taken up and before long the inevitable influx of Goilalas began. An entire settlement of Tuade speakers developed on the site complete with ceremonial ground-markers and a fence separating enemy clansmen who (through the eclectic use of kinship connections, which will be discussed in a later chapter) came to be urban neighbours.

When we happened to meet the lineage head whose offer began the whole process, he seemed appalled at what had occurred, bemoaning the fact that by befriending one man he now had dozens of houses on his land. And since the Goilalas have a fearsome reputation in Port Moresby, he is not likely to be evicting them either, although he hopes the government will help solve the problem.

The case has a further twist as the original native title to this particular plot of land is in dispute. The elder who allowed the first Goilala to settle actually felt that it might be in his interest to have someone living on the land who would back up his claim against that of another descent group. The courts will probably have a very difficult time deciding who really owns the land as Motu–Koita custom is flexible and based on oral tradition rather than written law. Until the issue is resolved, it is unlikely that any action can be taken against the Goilalas, which may be just as well, since the authorities seem to have no desire to force the settlers from their houses. Nevertheless, the situation is hardly a satisfactory one: the Goilalas are afraid that they will eventually be evicted, the local lineages see their land being gobbled up by people they fear and the government is faced with the uncontrolled proliferation of sub-standard dwellings with all their associated social, environmental and health problems.

In some towns (e.g. Mount Hagen) indigenous landholders do not permit migrants to establish houses on their land. In the Hagen area land is quite productive and used intensively. Local tribesmen are in a position of strength as their dense population outnumbers that of the town and they are very willing to fight. Squatters in Mount Hagen only build houses on government land, particularly patches that have not been built on because they happen to be very steep or on stream banks. In Port Moresby, however, where land is unproductive, indigenous population density low, and townsmen vastly outnumber locals (most of whom are employed in the urban economy), there is less pressure to hold land and less ability to dissuade migrants from building houses. Although particular land tenure problems do vary in this regard in different towns, and importantly affect relationships between the local population and migrants, each urban area has substantial tracts of migrant settlements. These have occasionally been cleared, but the general administrative response has been to allow migrant houses to lie in the gullies, near the creeks, under hillsides, outside boundaries, out of sight and out of mind.

In contrast to the manual worker who was seen as a temporary sojourner, some natives were gradually accepted as permanent residents by the authorities, especially as education and local political development proceeded. These people were provided with housing in planned areas which catered to families, or with a standard of single occupancy (in the case of clerks, students, police recruits, etc.) deemed suitable for those with needed skills.

The first planned areas were expatriate housing estates (locally known as high-covenant areas) which contained large European-style houses on substantial plots. The older high-covenant estates in each town had small servants' quarters attached to them and tended to be placed at a convenient distance from the ports or airstrips which were the foci of growth for central business districts. When housing estates for indigenes were built (smaller houses, with fewer amenities, on small plots) these were often located at a considerable distance from the central business district, making it difficult for residents to use urban facilities after working hours. Remaining land, often marginal for building purposes, and even farther from town centres, was used by 'squatters'. In some towns, however, migrant settlements may be found on some of the most centrally located land, especially if it is still in indigenous hands (Surmon 1971).

It was not until 1952 that suburbs were constructed for non-Europeans. In that year Gabutu in Port Moresby was erected for 'superior half- and quarter-castes (mixed bloods) and certain superior foreign natives', as well as a few 'completely detribalised Papuans' (Thompson, in Surmon 1971: 114). Even when more exclusively Papua New Guinean suburbs were built later on, the residents of these tended to be more highly paid than other indigenous wage-earners. In Hohola (also a Port Moresby suburb), for example, the average wage was double the average indigenous urban wage (Oeser 1969: 1–9).

In addition to having higher salaries than migrant settlers, better jobs, more education and a higher standard of living, these estate residents live in more multi-ethnic environments than those who build their own houses. They may also be closer to shops and other amenities than many settlement residents. On a superficial level, these areas look like the home of a developing middle class, while an underclass of seemingly tribalized natives live in the shanty towns and a mostly white upper class inhabits a tropical version of affluent western suburbia. Although this picture is extremely oversimplified as we shall see, it contains certain kernels of truth.

In keeping with the administrative function of the towns, many specialized educational institutions have been placed in them and a substantial number of barracks and dormitories have been erected for students. In addition, single workers' dwellings have been built by various companies for their skilled employees. These also resemble dormitories, contain a heterogeneous group of young, well-educated Papua New Guineans, and provide distinctly cosmopolitan settings where people of varied backgrounds interact frequently.

Colonial housing policy generally has kept expatriates and indigenes confined to separate housing areas. A late acceptance of Papua New Guineans as townsmen by Europeans meant that most early housing was provided for single men and after the war even that never kept pace with demand. Better accommodation for both families and skilled single people was built slowly as the administration set up training facilities for locals and began advances towards self-government. Indigenous housing estates, often far from town centres and European housing areas, catered for the more skilled native while a proliferation of educational and special-purpose training institutions created a fairly large dormitoried section of the urban population. A large leftover group of mainly unskilled manual workers were left to find their own solution to housing problems or provided with older and cruder barracks' spaces or servants' quarters. Racial residential segregation and incipient class separation can be readily seen from the air over any Papua New Guinea town.

As the pace of political change increased just prior to self-government and independence, the administration developed a less exclusive, more realistic housing policy and attempted to integrate suburbs. New areas were planned to combine indigenous market facilities, trade stores, supermarkets, high-covenant and low-covenant houses. As it became apparent that low-covenant housing was not going to be in the financial reach of many Papua New Guineans, tracts of land were set aside for 'no-covenant' areas where people from the settlements could relocate on land leased relatively cheaply from the government and build their own homes. These now secure residences could be gradually upgraded and provided with electricity, outdoor taps and basic sanitary services. Zoning rules, and restrictions on numbers of kin who could share contiguous plots, were seen as promoting controlled urban growth and tribal integration.

New suburbs being built in each town thus contain a much greater range of urban dwellers than previous ones. Within these, however, racial and economic segregation is still apparent as sub-areas for each housing type remain separate. Although higher level Papua New Guinean officials may now live next door to Europeans in high-covenant housing areas, low- and no-covenant areas have virtually no Europeans in them and are still predominantly the reserve of people with specific levels of income. Some of these suburbs are becoming new town centres, releasing the residents from dependence on private cars or rudimentary public transport for access to urban amenities.

Some remaining dimensions of marginality

Visitors to Papua New Guinea are sometimes surprised by the fact that urban facilities rarely reflect the traditional culture. Markets, which sell indigenously produced foodstuffs, and occasionally other items (such as clothing or artifacts), are an important exception to this generalization and they form meeting places for Papua New Guineans in every town. Churches, especially in coastal towns, have become locally controlled and are important foci of voluntary organizations. But their effectiveness as indigenous institutions is usually limited to the village area near any given town. Aside from markets and some churches, however, there is relatively little Papua New Guinean-style input into urban facilities or attractions. One cannot buy local food in a restaurant or on the street. Exotic eating places serve Chinese or Indonesian meals. Apart from the recent development of a national creative arts centre, there is no commercialized indigenous form of entertainment. People go to films, cinemas exist in every town, but these are owned by expatriates and show western movies. Even bars exclusively frequented by natives (the public hotel bars) are expatriate-owned. Each town has numerous clubs catering for specific sporting activities but these very often are either exclusively European or European-dominated. In the case of clubs organized around team sports such as rugby, cricket and softball, a considerable number of viable Papua New Guinean organizations exist. These are mainly formed by coastal men or women, as people from more recently contacted areas rarely belong to formal associations of any kind.

The relative absence of local-style businesses or organizations, especially in the formal economic sector, is indicative of the colonial forms still apparent in urban Papua New Guinea, and of the fact that access to western principles of organization, sources of business capital, etc., have been restricted. Although some Papua New Guineans have formed formal workers' or ethnic organizations, or entered into western-style businesses, the viability of these remains dependent on a very small number of men. As we shall see later, relatively few such enterprises are successful. The many voluntary associations which serve to aid urban migrants in various ways in Africa, Latin America and Asia, with their committees, officers and constitutions, are notable for their absence or marginality in Papua New Guinean towns. To acquire funds for business, funerals, etc., in urban areas, people usually rely on networks of kin and specific ethnic ties. While these networks may suffice for many purposes, they do restrict the potential for large indigenous pressure-groups to form. Although we have maintained that the Papua New Guinean man in the street has a substantial impact on the urban system, it is not manifested through formal control of urban resources but rather by working around and through the interstices of colonial style organizations. Despite the fact that an independent government now has control over urban development policy, there is a notable lack of middle-level pressure-groups that can serve to express the desires of common people and influence that policy.

Variations on a theme

Our theme in this chapter has been that a particular rural background and form of colonialism, the late development of towns, overall lack of industrialization and recency of entry by natives into alien environments, have set general conditions which have greatly affected urban development and the course of urbanization as a social process. Despite the fact that all towns in Papua New Guinea share the aforementioned general characteristics (which are especially apparent when they are compared to towns in other parts of the world), locally important urban differences do create a certain degree of variation.

Port Moresby, for example, is the largest urban centre in the country (containing 26 per cent of the national urban population) despite its virtual isolation from the most populous and economically dynamic parts of the nation. It is set in one of the most marginal food-producing areas of all of Melanesia and is in the ironic position of importing many foodstuffs from Queensland, Australia, which grow perfectly well in other parts of Papua New Guinea. If administration was not the prime urban industry, other centres would surely be larger than this one. But because of the centralization of administration and educational facilities, most businesses in the country maintain their head offices in Moresby, making the city a local business centre. Its very size and reputation make the capital the most talked-about town in the country and a magnet for migrants who associate 'Mosbi' with city life. This helps maintain the town's pre-eminence as a centre of indigenous urbanization.

We have already mentioned that Lae and the Highlands towns (Goroka, Kundiawa, Mount Hagen and Mendi), also administrative centres, are linked and form an important regional business network based on coffee and tea processing, transport and nascent industry. Other New Guinean towns (Rabaul, Madang and Wewak) are, like Moresby, somewhat cut off from other centres. Rabaul, the former capital of New Guinea, is located in the heart of an important cocoa and copra plantation area. But the town has been stagnating of late, as has Madang since the Highlands Highway diverted business with the interior from that port to

Lae. These centres seem destined to remain regional towns of moderate size, predominantly administrative, although Rabaul continues to be something of a centre of indigenous business enterprise and political consciousness. The remaining areas which are classifiable as urban are all provincial administrative towns with the exception of Arawa and Panguna which are urban areas built to house and serve people working for Bougainville Copper, by far the largest industry in Papua New Guinea. Conzinc Riotinto's huge mine has become the most important factor in Papua New Guinea's foreign trade and, with the attempted secession of Bougainville from the rest of the country (an issue which seems to have been resolved peacefully), helped create its most difficult political crisis. The typical association between urbanization and industrialization, very weak in the rest of the country, is strongest in south Bougainville.

Local economic developments and associated infrastructural, migratory, demographic and policy changes, will continue to cause greater specialization of urban function, urban growth and increased diversity, especially if new towns continue to be created around large-scale development projects of various sorts. (See Jackson (1976a) for fuller discussions of possible urban geographical trends.) This specialization may have less of an immediate effect on urbanization as a social process in Papua New Guinea, however, than in more industrialized countries. This is because Papua New Guineans are still predominantly unskilled, the economy is controlled by outside interests and most towns remain heavily administrative. If a man is an unskilled worker, his job as a cleaner for the government is virtually the same as another man's job as a cleaner for an industrial concern. The economic variation in urban centres will take on greater significance when local people become more dispersed throughout the socio-economic structure.

Of greater sociological importance at present, especially for the smaller towns, is the level of development of urban hinterlands, the composition of the urban population (especially the percentage of migrants from each region) and the nature of relations between local landholders and urban migrants.

Urban development requires land, brings a heterogeneous population into an area to fill urban roles and always fundamentally affects autochthonous populations. Even though various areas may face similar sorts of problems, these may bring forth different responses because of the environmental and historical peculiarities of each locale. These developmental and compositional differentials, a product of colonial experience as well as of aspects of the ecology of specific hinterlands, greatly affect local politics and ethnic idioms. Some examples will be discussed in a later chapter.

Our concentration on general developments in this chapter, although necessary to an understanding of urbanization in Papua New Guinea, is of course only part of the entire story. In terms of the goals set out in the introduction, the stage has merely been set, the actors hardly discussed. Although they live their lives in towns greatly influenced by their former expatriate masters, and accommodate to the demands of urban environments, Papua New Guineans are nevertheless creative within these contexts and construct their own social realities. In order to put the people more in focus, we consider the urban population itself in the next chapter.

3. Migration and the urban population

Population growth is a product of the interaction of three variables: fertility, mortality and migration. Between 1966 (the date of the first full urban census) and 1971, the overall population of Papua New Guinea's towns grew at an annual rate of 16.4 per cent. This brought the total urban population to 281,800, a rise from 4 to 9.5 per cent of the national population in five years (Papua New Guinea Census 1971). A small percentage of this growth was due to the inclusion of villages inside urban boundaries that had been outside in 1966, and about 2.5 per cent was the result of biological increase. The rest was due to urban migration. The magnitude of the migratory input into the populations of the main towns is so great that well over 50 per cent of the urban population was born outside the sub-districts in which the various towns were located. Port Moresby and Lae, the two largest towns, had 61 per cent and 62 per cent of their populations born outside their sub-districts. The south Bougainville towns had fully 84 per cent. Between a third and a half of all urban migrants (and up to 90 per cent for Arawa, Kieta and Panguna) arrived in the five-year period between the two censuses (May and Skelton 1975). Since urban population growth in Papua New Guinea is so much a result of migration, knowledge of the main trends in rural–urban movement is necessary to an understanding of urbanization as a social process.

The general pattern of migration

Most early wage-labour movement from any undeveloped area of Papua New Guinea was by contract, mostly to coastal plantations, many of which were near towns. Pre-war contract migrants were mainly from the Sepik, Gulf, Morobe, Madang and Milne Bay Districts. After the war, the Highlands became the main source for contract labour. This migration was usually circular, with provisions being made for repatriation and payment at home at the end of the contract period. Such arrangements allowed the administration to control the number of males absent from any area to a considerable extent. A good example of an agreement labour programme was the Highlands Labour Scheme run by the administration to provide workers for coastal areas (Harris 1974, May and Skelton 1975, M. Strathern 1975, Ward 1971, Department of Labour 1969).

26

In the 1950s some unskilled workers were sent to Port Moresby by the Highlands Labour Scheme, as well as to Sogeri (just outside the town) and Kokopo (close to Rabaul). These men were recruited by the administration personnel, given preventive medical treatment for coastal diseases, and dispatched to plantation or government works sites for two-year periods. A small number of workers decided to remain on the coast after their contracts were up or deserted, and moved into the nearest town to find work. Those who went home often spread fanciful tales of city life which encouraged others to join the scheme. Returnees sometimes used their repatriation pay to buy a ticket back to the coast a few months after their return. The desertion rate from a particular area tends to increase over time as a nucleus of people from there becomes established in various centres, providing a base for other people to attempt urban residence. The Highlands Labour Scheme was increasingly used as a free ride to the coast prior to its discontinuation in 1975. As time went on, its existence helped stimulate more people to come to towns independently of any formal contract.

The opening of regions for labour purposes and local economic development occur in sequence. As an area develops, and demand for cash grows, rural people shun low-paying plantation work and prefer to develop their own small businesses or seek better paid wage-labour in the towns. This tends to draw labour recruiters into less sophisticated areas where the process of shifting from contract migration to independent migration begins again. As the Highlands were opened in an east-to-west direction, most Highland migrants in coastal towns come from the Eastern Highlands, Chimbu and Western Highlands Provinces. Those working on the surrounding plantations tend to be from the less accessible areas of the Enga and Southern Highlands Provinces. By 1974, people from these areas were beginning to become established in Port Moresby, as Highlands Labour Scheme deserters and returnees established the seeds of an urban community.

A pattern of shifting from circular agreement to more independent chain migration has tended to develop throughout Papua New Guinea, with people from less developed areas arriving rather recently in large coastal centres. Following from this, the two crucial factors affecting the country's urban migration pattern are the specific history of contact and European penetration of various areas, and their distance from major European centres. Differences in these two variables explain much of the variation in local migration histories (May and Skelton 1975).

In very general terms, there has been a movement from densely populated interior regions to the New Guinea Islands (to plantations, Rabaul, and Bougainville mining towns) and to the coastal towns of Port Moresby, Lae, Madang and Wewak. The Gulf, Manus and Chimbu Provinces have the greatest rates of out-migration. Between 13 and 20 per cent of the people from these areas are now living outside them. Most Gulf people who leave home migrate to Port Moresby (60 per cent) or other towns, while most Chimbu tend to be rural–rural migrants (going into rural resettlement projects). Being the most densely populated province, however, makes even the relatively low proportion of rural–urban migrants among the Chimbu (25 per cent) significant for the towns. Slightly less than half of the Manus out-migrants wound up in the eight main urban centres (mentioned above), but as the district is small, they make a less visible impact than do the Chimbu.

Despite the movement from agreement to independent migration, circularity (returning home) remains prevalent. Slightly more than 50 per cent of the migrants returned home within the five-year period from 1966 to 1971 from the Central and Morobe Provinces (which contain Port Moresby and Lae). People from newly contacted areas (the Western and Southern Highlands, and the West Sepik) and Bougainville (because of opportunities created by the mine) most often go back to their province of origin. Only 15 per cent of the people from these provinces remained in one location between 1966 and 1971. (Many who went back to their village may return to urban areas in the future.)

As well as being the most residentially unstable urban migrants, people from more recently contacted areas tend to have the greatest ratio of male to female urbanites, partly because agreement work is mainly for males. Thus, longer-term residents with families in town tend to be from the more developed parts of Papua New Guinea. Despite these differences, rural–urban circulation is high from all areas and a fairly constant interchange of persons from town and country pertains (May and Skelton 1975).

Specific factors in urban migration

Particular conditions existing in the home area and at the migrants' destination, the way in which these are perceived, people's attitudes towards leaving their villages and their feelings about urban life in general, substantially affect population movements to towns. Among the factors cited in the local literature as affecting migration from specific areas are land pressure, rural income opportunities, the need for cash (for brideprice, tax, consumer goods), the desire to escape traditional obligations and authority, personal factors (arguments, etc.), the wish to acquire marketable skills or an education for one's children, boredom with village life, the attractions of the towns, availability of access to towns (roads, air services, coastal shipping), the desire to join urban resident kin, and the perception of migration as a rite of passage into manhood (Harris 1974). Particular variations in objective factors and in the perception of them result in different rates of migration as well as different patterns of urban involvement and rural–urban circulation.

Although most Papua New Guineans have adequate amounts of land for subsistence, land pressure is growing with rising population and increased cash-cropping. In areas where subsistence activities are most difficult and cash-cropping almost non-existent (parts of the Sepik, Gulf and Western Provinces), high rates of out-migration and relatively low rates of circularity pertain. For example, a tendency for Gulf migrants to remain in town, even when out of work, has been noted in Port Moresby (Hitchcock and Oram 1967: 105). Another study of Gulf migrants (the Toaripi studied by Ryan (1968)) stresses that many men leave home for good and establish families in urban areas. Those closest to home (in Port Moresby) maintain frequent contact with their villages, while Toaripi in Lae find this more difficult. Migration from Chimbu is also largely due to land shortage, but few if any people are actually forced to move to avoid starvation. In some places, like the Wosera area of the East Sepik Province, no correlation is found between population density and out-migration (Lea and Weinand 1971).

Some authors have noted that cash-cropping is negatively associated with migration in certain areas (e.g. Bedford and Mamak 1976, Harris 1972). Although it seems reasonable to suggest that rural development and cash-earning opportunities will decrease urban drift (Curtain 1975: 282–3), they may stimulate it as well through the subsequent growth of facilities (such as schools) which allow a greater diversification of options for earning money. Since much of the agricultural work in Papua New Guinea is done by women, men are relatively free to migrate *and* increase their cash-cropping activities if they leave wives at home to do weeding and harvesting.

A linear relationship between cash-cropping and out-migration is probably too simplistic. Salisbury and Salisbury (1972), for example, report that Sianes likely to leave the Eastern Highlands for Port Moresby usually do not come from the most or least developed parts of their territory, but from an intermediary zone, where cash-cropping is difficult but enables one to earn enough money for the air-fare. M. Strathern (1972) has noted a similar pattern for Hagen migrants to Port Moresby.

Easy access to regional centres or larger towns (for employment or markets) seems to obviate the need for migration. Outside this zone, however, absenteeism is closely correlated with distance from a town. This is obvious from the census data which show that most migrants to any town (about two-thirds) are from an adjacent province or region. Nevertheless, migration from distant areas to most towns is increasing at a faster rate than overall migration (May and Skelton 1975).

Different towns also have different attractions for migrants. Hagens, for example, do not like to go to Lae because it is too easily reached by relatives (M. Strathern 1975). Orokaiva, on the other hand, prefer the more accessible Lae and Highlands centres to Moresby when they leave the Northern Province (Baxter 1973). Urban development itself also creates 'pulls' for migrants. Bougainville Copper has attracted people from all over Papua New Guinea to the Arawa–Kieta–Panguna area where most of the population is made up of recent migrants. Lae and Goroka have also grown quickly with the completion of the Highlands Highway. Rabaul, however, seems to be drawing proportionately fewer recent migrants than the aforementioned towns because of general commercial stagnation.

An issue which has received a lot of attention is individual motives for migration to towns. A number of authors (e.g. Conroy 1972, Curtain 1975, Salisbury and Salisbury 1970), as well as the migrants themselves, stress the economic aspects of their move. Towns are often represented as places where money is easy to get, many people emphasizing that exaggerated accounts of its availability tempted them into migrating. But desire for wage-work is not evidence that an individual expects to remain an urbanite indefinitely. Various researchers have noted that unskilled migrants view themselves as temporary urban dwellers in town to acquire capital or skills for a rural business. This seems particularly true of Highlanders who place a high value on rural entrepreneurial activity (Conroy and Curtain 1973, Harris 1972, Salisbury and Salisbury 1972). The circularity of Highlands migration noted above tends to be consistent with this general attitude.

Nevertheless, well-educated migrants, no matter what area they come from, tend to be more career-oriented than the unskilled. Those with training relevant to positions only pursuable in towns feel they are more likely to remain urbanites for their working lives, and perhaps present us with the clearest motives for migration. These entail more than just economic rationality though, as desires for a Western life-style are also stressed. Many of these skilled individuals say they plan to retire to their villages and eventually live off the proceeds of rural businesses. Their ultimate plans are therefore somewhat similar to those of their less skilled brothers, but they do tend to remain in towns for longer periods of time.

An emerging phenomenon of some importance is the tendency for school-leavers who have not acquired any marketable western skills to be dissatisfied with the village life. Papua New Guinea's recent colonial education system was in itself (and perhaps still is) an ideological preparation for a non-traditional life-style (Curtain 1975: 274–81). People with no formal education tend to see themselves as temporarily absent from home. The skilled are prepared to adopt non-village residence for their working lives. But students who leave school after Standard Six (after six years of primary school) are caught in between. Fruitlessly aspiring towards a life-style impossible for them to achieve because of their lack of skills and certification, the school-leavers in a town are over-represented in the urban unemployed (Conroy 1973), but are less willing than the unschooled to accept roles consistent with village life. Their presence and lack of success in the urban environment is one of Papua New Guinea's fastest growing problems.

Although economic motives are so frequently put forward by migrants of all types, we should avoid the tendency towards attributing too much explanatory power to them. Rew (1974), for example, has noted that workers in a Port Moresby company from various areas and different levels of skill manifest significant ambivalence towards the ways in which city people make money. Even while working in Port Moresby they accord rural occupations considerable prestige and plan to return to their villages, typically expressing some disillusionment with city life. A number of our own informants from the general Siane area, like the Salisburys', said that they came to Port Moresby to get money or learn skills needed to run rural businesses. But aside from a few who took driving lessons, no one seemed even to come close to realizing these ambitions. Ironing clothes, washing floors and cutting grass, tasks which engaged the majority of these individuals, were neither potentially useful skills nor paid more than a subsistence wage. Yet they continued to stay in Moresby or come back after brief visits home because they were, as they put it, 'bored with village life'.

The most notable critique of the 'economic man' image of urban migration in Papua New Guinea comes from M. Strathern (1975; forthcoming). She feels her Hagen informants' statements about coming to Moresby to 'find money' are simply *ex post facto* rationalizations for a more complex set of motivations. Like some other people in Papua New Guinea, Hageners place a high value on rural entrepreneurship which they combine with a vigorous scorn of urban wage-labour. Wealth in Hagen eyes is to be deployed strategically, through exchange, to raise the status of individuals and groups. 'Eating money' by paying for consumer goods, rent, food, etc., is considered wasteful, yet urban men spend almost all their money in this way. Unskilled workers returning home rarely bring enough money back to cover their debts to those who looked after their land or pigs while they were away. Since their age-mates have already started establishing themselves by getting married and planting coffee trees, returnees often find they have lost considerable status by having been away. Their desire to 'find money' in the town and the stress on economic factors may really be most relevant to why they *stay*, as opposed to why they *left*. Without a lot of money to bring home, those migrants who have spent more than a few years in town may stay on to avoid returning to a subordinate position or low-status situation in the village.

One may wonder why they left home in the first place. Strathern notes that most Hagen migrants in Moresby are young bachelors (16–25 years old) who have not yet started cash-cropping or whose coffee trees have not yet matured. She sees many as prolonging their periods of adolescent freedom from adult responsibilities. Migrants themselves stress their immaturity and unimportance in the urban (unskilled) Hagen community. Other men have left their villages because of boredom, troubles of various sort, or a desire to experience a new way of life.

A number of other studies show that in other areas wage-labour is not as looked down upon as it is in Hagen. The Isivita Orokaiva (Baxter 1973) value returnees' experience and may accord them leadership roles in introduced activities. The Sio of the Vitiaz Straits are reported to prefer wage-work to cash-cropping. Even though they can make more at home, they view wage-work as easier, they like the fact that money comes in more quickly and feel that too much cash-cropping prevents full participation in village activities while living at home (Harding 1971). Other authors report that men are expected to migrate since a lack of warfare gives them little scope to prove their manhood or establish prestige (Baxter 1973, Harris 1972, Zimmerman 1973). Even though attitudes towards wage-labour may be positive in some areas, the ramifications of Strathern's argument go beyond Hagen.

The entire 'economic' versus 'social' (or 'city lights') issue is predicated on a false dichotomy as a number of scholars now realize. Those who stress investment motives have overly concentrated on the statements of migrants and have not provided data on actual amounts of money saved and deployed in rural businesses or on specific skills acquired. The actual relationship between the job market's dynamics and fluctuations and urban migration is not understood in Papua New Guinea (May and Skelton 1975). Aside from these objections, the desire for money and the ambition to obtain it in certain ways are very much related to specific ideas about status and perceptions of rural potential and urban life. Migration is a multi-faceted phenomenon and is a function of objective factors (such as distance from a town), subjective factors (cultural attitudes towards status and perceptions of urban and rural life-styles and opportunities), as well as purely personal factors of individual circumstances. Despite the great room for variation in the combination of these factors, the general trends discussed above stand out clearly, as does the simple observation that once individuals from a specific area reach a town, others from that same area tend to join them in increasing numbers (ibid.).

Migration and urban ideology

As was stressed above, migration is a part of the overall process of 'modernization'. Differences in the experience of development within the rural population are the cause of variation in the past and present patterns of spatial and socio-economic mobility. These assume great importance as far as specific differentiation within the urban population is concerned. From a more detached perspective, however, urban migration in Papua New Guinea is a relatively recent phenomenon and this has certain general implications for the entire urban population.

At this point in time, urban migration has not led to great rural–urban disjunctions. As we have seen, most townsmen are first-generation migrants and rural–urban circulation is high. Although a considerable number of men from some communities may be absent in town, the effects of this on the village may be compensated for by a number of factors. The Hula, for example, do not leave dependants at home for others to care for (Oram 1968). Isivita Orokaiva remittances from town help the rural people, who do not seem adversely affected by the 30 per cent absentee rate (Baxter 1973: 10). The young Hageners who migrate have little productive role in the village. Even when older men from the Highlands areas leave, they cause relatively little strain on the village community because their wives take care of the cash-crops and they either send money home or visit periodically. The large number of young Sio working away from home also send money back and return when middle-aged to responsible positions in the community (Harding 1967). In such circumstances, urban migration is not disastrous for the village.

In those areas where out-migration is greatest and circulation least frequent we might expect greater rural dislocation. Indeed, migration to Port Moresby has so depleted some Gulf Province areas that gardening has stopped in places of static or declining population, and settlements have broken up as people scatter to collect wild sago (Brookfield 1960: 271). But according to one full-length study of Gulf migrants from the Toaripi area, 'there is a bi-local social system with town dwellers and village dwellers equally members' (Ryan 1970: 1). This same complementarity of the rural and urban, the movement back and forth and the unity of town and village, is frequently stressed by researchers and informants from all over the country. The writings of those social scientists who stress the contrasts, disjunctions and separateness of the rural and urban spheres seem overdrawn in the context of the Papua New Guinea experience. What Baxter states for the Isivita Orokaiva, that 'the town is a vital and integral part of the village world' (1973: 111), is true of other areas as well. Indeed, Ryan and Oram stress that there is one network of social relations which ties migrants together with home people. Ryan may have a valid point in viewing Toaripi society as a 'bi-local social system'. From the perspective of any particular set of migrants, separating that bi-local system into two different spheres may seem arbitrary. But from a less mono-ethnically bounded viewpoint, there is ample justification for discussing urban social fields as systems in their own right.

It is important to stress that home orientation or 'rurally oriented strategies' are very much a part of this urban system and have great implications for urban behaviour, attitudes, groupings, etc., which will come out in more detail later. At this point we should note that in addition to being reflected in individual migration choices, in chain migration and in exchanges of news, persons, money, etc., between town and village, rural interests also tend to keep migrants from the same area involved in social networks which are largely made up of home people. Rather than look upon rural orientation as evidence of a lack of urban commitment, we should explore its implications for urban social life. When Hageners talk about home links, for example, 'They are emphasizing their common cultural origins and the rationale for town based relationships and also the extent to which their interests as migrants differentiate them from members of the rural society' (M. Strathern, forthcoming).

This interdependence of the urban and rural may coexist with ideologies of independence sometimes directed at the town, and sometimes at the home area or its representatives in town (ibid.). Despite a difficult employment market, Papua New Guineans seem very willing to leave jobs with which they are dissatisfied. Rather than desperately hanging on in the face of adversity, people often tend to move in and out of employment, stressing their ability to go home or receive aid from home people while looking for a better situation. On other occasions, urbanites stress their independence from rural concerns when these may interfere with urban pursuits. Tribal animosities are sometimes played down with the comment, 'That's a village affair, we're here to work not fight.' Demands of kin may be shrugged off as the urbanite portrays himself as being in an alternative social system. Overplaying either independence from the town or from kin can lead to urban failure. One would either leave for home in the one case or become cut off from a valuable base of support on the other. However, the complementary and selective use of these ideologies of independence can promote urban adjustment. Because most migrants have little security other than that provided by their kin in town, to assert a certain distance from their marginal economic situation prevents some of the despair and palliates the unpleasantness of low urban socio-economic status. Likewise, the excessive demands of home people can be held off by accentuating one's urban commitments. These ideologies ultimately grow out of the historical and developmental matrix we have been stressing all along. They are quite clearly continuous with and reinforced by the attitudes and experiences of urban migration which involve Papua New Guineans in new environments while simultaneously encouraging them to remain attached to home people.

The urban population: developing differentiation

As we might expect, the various factors involved in creating patterns of urban migration affect not only the composition of the urban population but the developing pattern of urban socio-economic differentiation. In this section we discuss some of the main aspects of urban population composition and differentiation (see Garnaut, forthcoming, Levine 1976).

It was already mentioned that 281,000 people, 9.5 per cent of the nation's population, lived in urban areas in 1971, an annual increase of 16.4 per cent since 1966. We also know that most of these people are the first-generation townsmen and that there is a preponderance of single males. The demographic disproportion of the urban population (its difference from the national composition) has been decreasing; since 1966 the number of men in towns has doubled, but the number of women increased by 250 per cent. They now make up 38.2 per cent of the urban population. The urban population remains skewed in the direction of those of working age. Fully one-quarter of the country's males between 15 and 44 years old live in towns where they make up 50 per cent of the urban population. The overall trend in the age structure of the male population is also moving towards greater similarity to the national population. In fact, with the present age and sex structure, the birth rate in towns should approximate that of the country as a whole, although the urban population is likely to have an over-representation of younger males for some time. These demographic movements towards greater rural–urban parity strongly indicate an increasing tendency towards urban family formation which can be expected to result in more long-term residence for many Papua New Guineans.

The towns with the greatest tendency to mirror the rural population demographically are those (like Wewak and Rabaul) within whose boundaries fall the most urban villages. The mining centres of Bougainville, on the other hand, are filled with single males. Some of the differences between towns reflects administrative zoning, but the rapid industrialization of south Bougainville is the cause of the demographic situation there. In general, it is those towns that attract migrants from far afield which have the most pronounced demographic differences from the national population. This is because of the fact that in the less developed areas, farther from the towns, the first migrants are invariably males of working age, especially if contract labour is the main form of migration.

Distance from a town and recency of migration also creates demographic differences for various ethnic and regional sections of a specific town's population. In Port Moresby, for example, the general male to female ratio is 1.5:1. But for Highlanders in Moresby there are almost six males to every female. In Mount Hagen, however, the male:female ratio for Highlanders is about the same as the overall town ratio (1.45:1) (Papua New Guinea Census 1971).

As we shall see below, the lower likelihood for Highlanders in coastal towns to have normal family circumstances is paralleled by their marginal position in other spheres of urban life. As part of the process of urban social differentiation, this marginality is an important aspect of social change. But we should stress that this differentiation is a relatively recent phenomenon. Most Papua New Guineans are still unskilled as far as urban sector employment is concerned no matter where in the country they come from.

Some perspective on this is gained when we note that over 95 per cent of the urban population over the age of 10 has not completed any formal job training programme (an apprenticeship course, intermediate certificate or tertiary education programme). In Port Moresby, the national capital and centre for such programmes, less than 3 per cent of the urban population had such formal credentials. Only 1.2 per cent obtained a leaving certificate and 46 per cent did not complete even one year of school. Yet it is participation in the urban economy, primarily as workers, that most effectively brings urbanites into a new system of social relations and behavioural patterns. As a result of political changes and the official policy of 'localization' of the labour force (replacing expatriates with nationals), Papua New Guineans are now beginning to appear in a greater range of occupations than ever before. The majority of workers remain in unskilled or semi-skilled jobs, however, and the numbers of skilled or professional people are quite small. Although urban economic diversification may be expected to grow, the greatest single urban employer (the majority employer in some towns) remains the government. Relatively few Papua New Guineans find themselves in the position of being factory workers. This lack of a numerically large industrial proletariat is one factor which affects the type of class consciousness and union activity one encounters in urban Papua New Guinea. We will, however, discuss the urban employment situation and its implications in greater detail in Chapter Five.

A large number of people living in the seven major urban areas (Port

Moresby, Lae, Rabaul, Madang, Wewak, Goroka and Mount Hagen) are not involved in formal sector work. From 15 to 25 per cent of the males of working age, and 80 to 90 per cent of the females, were not working for wages in 1973. At first glance this would seem like an enormous unemployment problem, even in comparison with the western countries hardest hit during the latest world economic crisis. But in Papua New Guinea it seems that a substantial proportion of those not working are not seeking jobs and should not be counted as unemployed. In Goroka, for example, about 20 per cent of those of working age are voluntarily outside the formal sector: they are living in villages included in the town boundary, but are either engaged in subsistence activities, or just visiting, occasionally selling produce, etc. A large proportion of urban women tend to sell garden produce in markets, or try to gain money by gambling, as these activities are compatible with looking after children. Overall, from 8.5 to about 20 per cent of the urban population of the seven major towns do not seek to enter the formal sector.

Subtracting those voluntarily not working, the true unemployment rate (those actively seeking or wanting immediate work) varies from 5 to 12 per cent. Very few of these unemployed people are trapped in the town. Those who do not have work and would like to go home, but cannot, make up from 0.2 to 1.5 per cent of the urban male population and 0.0 to 5.5 per cent of the female population. This provides evidence that most of the unemployed can rely on kin and friends until they do find work. The fact that virtually everyone has a rural option also means that not having a job is less of a personal disaster in Papua New Guinea than it is in countries where the option does not exist. The overall rate of population and job turnover that pertains in the towns makes it likely that most people experience relatively frequent periods of unemployment and may often change their minds as to whether or not they wish to enter the formal sector. The survey from which the figures quoted above were taken (reported in Wright (1975)) would only give one a static picture of the job scene, although it forms a necessary base for future studies. In general it seems that the urban ideology and pattern of rural–urban movements discussed above are reflected in a fluid employment situation.

Although the figures available were not broken down further than the report of general trends given above, a number of studies of specific urban migrant groups show an expected tendency for those from undeveloped areas (who tend to be unskilled and uneducated) to have the lowest employment rates. The relatively skilled Hula in Port Moresby refuse unskilled work but seem to have no trouble finding jobs. Only 3 per cent are unemployed (Oram 1968: 18). The (mostly Gumine) Chimbu who live in the Six-Mile rubbish-dump migrant settlement have a 27 per cent unemployment rate. Other studies in Port Moresby show that about 16 per cent of the Siane (Eastern Highlands), 20–39 per cent of Gulf District migrants, about 5 per cent of the Orokaiva (but 35 per cent in Lae) and 9 per cent of the Hagens are unemployed (summarized in Harris 1974). The usefulness of these figures for comparative purposes is diminished by the variable definitions of employment and unemployment used by the different fieldworkers and the fact that the studies were done at different times. More controlled census data does, however, exist which allows us to discern trends in urban socio-economic differentiation for people from different areas.

When we break down figures for formal qualifications, education and newness to town, by region of origin, it becomes clear that chances for success in the urban environment are differentially distributed among people from different parts of the country. Papua New Guinea is commonly divided into four regions: Papua, the Highlands, the New Guinea Islands and New Guinea Coast. These categories often become foci of ethnic conflict in the towns, especially when regional inequalities are stressed. In most towns, New Guinea Islanders and Papuans are the most educated and qualified for skilled positions, with Highlanders being far and away the least qualified. In Mount Hagen, for example, 18.5 per cent of the Islanders, 7.4 per cent of Papuans, 3 per cent of the New Guinea Coastals and only 0.7 per cent of the Highlanders have formal job certification. In Port Moresby the regions fall in the same rank order although the differences are less pronounced (9.3, 1.9, 1.7 and 0.7 per cent). Highlanders are also the newest urbanites (as was mentioned in the migration section), even in Highland towns (Levine 1976).

Being least educated or qualified, Highlanders are concentrated in the lowest-paying jobs, positions which are the least secure and hold the fewest opportunities for advancement. As we pointed out before, they are least likely to have their wives or children in town and tend not to reside in one urban area continuously. The Islanders and Papuans, who are best prepared for the urban economy, are from areas which have long been in contact with Europeans and have benefited from mission or colonial education systems. New Guinea Coastals have generally benefited less than Papuans and Islanders in terms of educational development.

A pattern of regional socio-economic differentiation is developing in urban Papua New Guinea with Coastals (especially Papuans and Islanders) in the most privileged positions and Highlanders in the least. Such patterns mask internal differences within regions, but it is the overall pattern that assumes greatest significance in urban ethnic conflict. Specific variations are likely to be ignored when regional stereotypes come to the fore. Although this trend is just developing it may be expected to intensify. As the colonial dichotomy of racial differentiation (which created black–white social, economic and political inequality) fades, Papua New Guineans are moving higher up the social ladder. After the country has become 'localized', with young coastal men dominating positions of responsibility, further mobility will probably lessen, and the class and regional system of inequality stabilize.

Conclusion

In this chapter we have seen how certain phenomena relating to colonization, rural development and the wider national context have generally affected the composition, ideology and developing pattern of socio-economic differentiation of the urban population. These aspects of urban environments are, of course, more specific manifestations of those general factors that were discussed in the previous chapter. Stressing the generation of these aspects of urbanization puts that process in a wider context (cf. Rollwagen 1975) and allows us to explain and understand urban social action more fully than would a discussion which proceeded as if the towns were closed systems. Because the urban system itself is part of a wider social field, urban behaviour cannot be considered as entirely *sui generis*. As we move more deeply into an analysis of urban society itself, the influence of that wider field which has affected the formation and peopling of Papua New Guinea's towns will be seen to be continually present, setting constraints and incentives to urban social behaviour.

4. Security: primary social relationships in town

It should be obvious from the foregoing discussion that becoming established in a Papua New Guinean town is by no means a purely personal affair. As was mentioned previously, various urban features such as the general housing shortage, lack of comprehensive social welfare provisions, difficulties of getting a job, and the presence of strangers and tribal enemies, set substantial adjustment problems for a newly urban population characterized by a low level of urban relevant skills and experience. In such circumstances people are dependent on a wider circle of others than the average resident of a western town. Papua New Guineans commonly attempt to surround themselves with a substantial base of personal support to cope with urban life, not only upon initial arrival but throughout their stay in town. In this chapter we examine the sorts of choices people make in recruiting others to their social networks, and the kinds of relationship patterns and social situations that result from these choices.

Two interrelated sets of factors seem to enter into the production of these patterns. They are facilitated by the use of certain social categories and affected by various concrete aspects of the urban system, particularly by characteristics of the urban residential domain. The interaction of these social idioms and urban residential contingencies produce both general processes of relationship throughout the towns and more specific domestic and community forms centred in various housing areas among people of different rural background.

Because neighbourhoods provide an anchoring point, and the first task of a new urbanite is to find a place to stay, we will start our discussion of the formation of primary relationships in terms of their urban location. This provides an opportunity for descriptions of urban neighbourhoods which add to our general picture of local town life, and also furnish a background for the more abstract discussion of the operation of some important social categories which follows.

The residential domain

A detailed description of how urban Papua New Guineans go about their ordinary everyday lives would need to draw upon a substantial body of urban ethnographic data. But although surveys of employment patterns, eating habits, household budgets, demographic composition, etc., have been conducted in a number of different settlements, very few in-depth studies of any urban neighbourhoods exist. Nevertheless, in the next few sections we will try to integrate the surveys and observational data that are available in order to give the reader at least some of the flavour of life in the towns' residential areas. We will also compare the various types of neighbourhoods with a view towards ascertaining their influence on the residents' social relationships.

The proportions of urbanites living in the different sorts of residential situations varies from town to town. For example, in Mount Hagen well over half the indigenous population lives in squatter-type dwellings, while in the Bougainville mining towns less than 10 per cent do so (Jackson 1976b). But taking the indigenous urban population as a whole, it has been estimated that close to half of all townsmen live in urban villages and settlements and this proportion is expected to increase substantially in the future (Jackson 1977: 25–6).

These urban villages and settlements tend to be mono-ethnic in character or made up of large mono-ethnic sub-sections. As such, they are often the focus of the sorts of networks of primary relationships vital to an urbanite's personal security and comfort. They will provide an appropriate starting point for our discussion of neighbourhoods as the context for the development and maintenance of such relationships.

Urban settlements

The urban settlements have tended to have something of a reputation for squalor and social disorganization, particularly with colonial administrators and expatriate residents. Indeed, one would not expect living conditions to be ideal where past administrations have denied the settlements water, sewage and rubbish collection services in a vain attempt to discourage migration to the towns. The visual impact is typically that of a collection of rough plank sheds or native-material huts, with roofs made of corrugated metal scraps held down with a few large stones. They are laid out in no apparent pattern – certainly not in the orderly rows which expatriates seem to appreciate.

But the corresponding image of these neighbourhoods as the home of single, unemployed men – parasites who only drink and steal – is not an accurate one. As we pointed out in Chapter Two, the main impetus for migrants to build their own homes in these settlements was the sheer inadequacy of the housing provided by the administration and other employers, particularly for their married workers and their families. So although there are certainly a number of single men living in the settlements, the households are largely built around nuclear families, as the figures below will illustrate.

A study of a canoe settlement in Port Moresby found that every household (save the researcher's) consisted of a nuclear family with or without the addition of a few relatives of the husband or wife (Oram 1967: 25). Only one man was not employed. Among the Purari Delta people living in Rabia Camp settlement in Port Moresby, each household had one nuclear family while 11 per cent of the men were unemployed (Hitchcock and Oram 1967: 56, 63). A survey of Nuigo settlement in Wewak found that 9 per cent of the households were entirely composed of adult men (i.e. all the rest had at least one nuclear family), but the men in these households only made up 5 per cent of the population of the settlement. Very similar figures were reported from Boundary Road settlement in Lae, where 9 per cent of the households, representing 6 per cent of the settlement's population, were composed of men only. In Ranuguri, a long-standing settlement in Port Moresby, such households made up just 4 per cent of the settlement structure and 2 per cent of its population (Allen *et al.* 1975, Department of Geography, University of Papua New Guinea 1974, Jackson and Forbes 1975, summarized in Jackson 1976b and 1977: 31).

The overall employment situation in these settlements is less than ideal, but there is an average of between one and two wage-earners per household in each (1.2 in Nuigo, 1.6 in Boundary Road, 1.9 in Ranuguri and 1.7 in Corners settlement in Daru). Only a small proportion of households find themselves without a resident wage-earner at any one time (6, 2, 4 and 3 per cent respectively) (Jackson 1976b: 60). Levels of unemployment and the presence of migrants' wives and families in specific settlements tends to vary, of course, with the particular group of migrants and their particular situation in the town as a whole.

These demographic and employment statistics provide little more than a glimpse of what life is like in the urban settlements. We can fill this bare outline in somewhat by referring to the available urban ethnographies.

Most anthropologists who have done urban research in Papua New Guinea have tended to focus on a particular ethnic group whose members had migrated to the town rather than on urban forms *per se* (e.g. Ryan 1970, Strathern 1975, Zimmerman 1973). Where the anthropologist has also spent a significant period of fieldwork in the group's home area, it is not surprising to find a particular interest in rural–urban continuities. While this perspective has limitations for dealing with urbanization in general, it will allow us to look at certain aspects of urban social life and the residential milieus these authors have studied.

In a dissertation on the Buang people living in Lae, Zimmerman describes the all-Buang settlement of Three-Mile as being entirely village-like (1973: 85). Town life is said to be little different from that of the village (ibid.: 91) since Buangs make their houses and activities as home-like as possible (ibid.: 9). She actually goes so far as to state that 'In many ways it is foolish to talk of "urbanisation" for the New Guinean since the migrant transports village surroundings, habits, foods, customs and language to whatever destination is his goal, whether it be an urban centre or another village' (ibid.: 18). Zimmerman argues that Buangs are not true urbanites since they neither participate in town-based institutions nor contribute to the ongoing quality of the urban setting or its survival (ibid.: 14–15). Although she acknowledges that there are also important differences in that men are engaged in wage-labour and women relieved of the hard work of village subsistence gardens, Zimmerman points out that it is not absolutely necessary to have a job in town (because one can count on the support of fellow migrants) and that the family life of these townsmen has survived largely intact.

Zimmerman's emphasis on the similarities between urban settlement and village life is not based solely on the existence of houses that look like village houses or the eating of the same sorts of foods (a combination of European and native comestibles) that are consumed in the village. Convergence goes beyond a superficial similarity of life-styles to an essential continuity between town and village that has become a basic part of Buang society and culture.

Within the urban settlements, family and village relationships continue to be important. Households tend to be shared between kinsmen. Buang migrants depend upon each other for help and support and are largely isolated from other townsmen. They attend church in Buang groups, drink with other Buangs, and even withdrew from a credit union because they were not allowed to form their own separate branch.

In addition, there is a strong preference among Buang girls (who seem to pick their own spouses) for marrying townsmen. While they tend to be separated from the youths who have gone to town to look for work during the courting years, young Buang women often visit their relatives in town, usually for short periods, and in this way keep in touch with the young male migrants. The men, if they have a job and a place to live, send home for a village girl to marry. Thus, migration has become almost a prerequisite to getting a wife, and spending one's young adult years in the town is seen as a normal part of Buang life. The migrants, like men from other areas, speak in terms of earning money in the town to invest in village businesses and returning to enjoy their later years in the village.

Ryan also greatly emphasizes continuities with the village in her study of Toaripi-speakers living in an urban settlement in Port Moresby, suggesting that migrants and villages form a single bi-local system. The Toaripi households in Vabukori settlement seem to have formed along lines of village-based kinship and, according to Ryan, the settlement actually functions as a village in many ways. Kinship ties involve the settlement dwellers in networks of reciprocal obligation that result in the sharing of housing, food, money and services. Residents of Vabukori are deeply involved in village affairs. Important decisions, disputes and celebrations may involve both villagers and settlement dwellers (Ryan 1968: 62–6).

Hageners living in Port Moresby have not developed the sort of village-like communities reported above. Migration from their part of the Western Highlands District is considerably smaller in numbers and scale, more recent and male-dominated than for the Toaripi and Buang. Also, Hageners traditionally live in scattered hamlets on clan lands rather than in nucleated villages (M. Strathern 1975).

In Port Moresby we find no substantial Hagen residential centres. Hageners live dispersed in various settlements and resettlement areas, domestic quarters, barracks and low-covenant houses. Despite such scattering, certain individual Hagen households seem to have taken on some of the characteristics of rural men's houses (where men traditionally live together away from their wives). This sort of urban domestic arrangement is only possible if the Hagen householder is living in some sort of urban settlement or resettlement area. A similar type of household may also be maintained in domestic quarters and company-provided housing if the employer does not object to lots of friends and relatives being around. A number of people (usually of the same clan but sometimes matrilateral or affinal relations) move in with the migrant, and the household attracts visitors. It may then become something of a recreation centre, typically associated with a particular clan or tribal group, a place where the migrants can exchange news, gossip, play cards, eat, drink and spend leisure time together (ibid.: 202).

But there are some differences as well. For instance, even where the migrants from a particular part of the country are described as being centralized in a 'village-like' settlement, the population of that settlement will be much more diverse than that of their village. Although the ethnic group may represent something of a united front to the rest of the town, within the mono-ethnic urban settlements (or within a major mono-ethnic section of a large multi-ethnic settlement) it is common to find that the houses form clusters that correspond to the village of origin or other traditional grouping of the residents. However much settlement dwellers may share the same language and other cultural traits, they also recognize differences among themselves, often on clan, sub-clan or village lines. Since a new migrant characteristically moves in with a kinsman if at all possible, most households are composed of members of the same kin group or village (plus affines). When a man builds his own house, it will often be next door to a clan brother's. But people may activate matrilineal and affinal ties as well, and thus clusters of houses from different villages or clans are often found within a settlement (Levine 1976, Oram 1967: 22, Ryan 1970: 76–84).

Ivane settlement in Port Moresby provides a particularly clear illustration of this phenomenon. The households of the residents (who are from the Goilala area of the Central Province) tend to be composed of clan brothers, and when the early settlers obliged their brothers-in-law by allowing them to build houses in the settlement, clusters of houses on kin and affinal lines developed. The Goilala (as is common in Papua New Guinea) tend to marry into groups with which they have relationships of traditional enmity. This provides a certain amount of contact as well as some cross-cutting ties between enemies. When we visited Ivane urban settlement in 1972, tribal fighting was no longer going on in that part of the country, but nevertheless, disputes within the settlement cropped up between members of the enemy clans and seemed seriously to disrupt relationships between them. At the time we were there, it would hardly have been necessary to ask each householder what clan he belonged to in order to map out the clusters or 'territory' of the enemy groups, since the residents had actually put a barbed-wire fence down the middle of the settlement to separate themselves (Levine 1976).

Thus, although there are many continuities between life in the urban settlements and the villages from which these townsmen come, we cannot get a complete picture of the settlements by concentrating solely on their village-like aspects. The contingencies of the town force the migrants to make many departures from village ways and forms.

Another change from village life-styles is the typical overcrowding of the houses in the settlements. Housing is scarce in most urban areas of Papua New Guinea, at least in part because of the colonial administration's efforts to discourage migration, but also because there is a limited amount of land in the urban centres. As we mentioned earlier, programmes are under way to provide more housing and upgrade existing settlements (through the provision of such amenities as sewage, water, latrines, street lighting, as well as secure land tenure), but it will be many years (if ever) before facilities can properly catch up with the growing urban population (Jackson 1976b: 65). This is particularly so where (as in nearly every major town) most of the suitable land for the expansion of housing is under customary tenure, i.e., owned by the local indigenous population, who are increasingly loath to part with it. The housing pinch is felt severely in the urban settlements, and indeed we find that their occupancy rate is estimated at 6.9 residents per household on the average as opposed to 5.6 for other types of neighbourhoods (Jackson 1977: 25).

Zimmerman points to the crowding in Buang households in Lae as one of the aspects of urban settlement life that is particularly different from the village. She found that in Lae, where there is an exceptionally severe shortage of housing, there was a much greater tendency for extended families to be living together (1973: 85).

Ryan noted that Toaripi-speakers in Lae were also especially likely to be living in extended and multi-family households, and that furthermore, the members of such a household would tend to form a tight little network within which they would share food and child-care responsibilities, as well as exchanging other goods and services (1970: 85).

Extended families and multiple nuclear families are fairly common features of urban settlements in general. In the canoe settlement of Badili, Port Moresby, five out of fourteen households were made up of extended families, some including more than one nuclear family (Oram 1967: 25). In Nuigo settlement, Wewak, the proportion of such households is 55 per cent; in Boundary Road settlement, Lae, the proportion is 65 per cent; and in Ranuguri settlement, Port Moresby, 67 per cent (Jackson 1976b: 58).

Thus extended family households, although formed on traditional principles of kinship and affinity, may be seen (at least for some groups) to be distinctly urban formations. In fact, we should look at the urban settlements in general as indigenous adaptations to the urban environment. The use of rural idioms has resulted in many continuities with the village, in terms of life-style, marriage patterns and the evidence of traditional principles of social organization in the very formation of the households and the settlements as a whole. At the same time, these rural idioms and principles, interacting with the constraints of the urban environment (such as scarcity of land and housing), have led to certain basic differences exemplified by the extended family households and the mixture of members of different traditional groups that live together in the settlements.

Different from the village as it may be, the urban settlement has nevertheless taken on some of its functions, again adapted to the constraints and necessities of the urban environment. Many settlements are staging areas for important traditional occasions such as funeral feasts and other ceremonials. But in the town there may be the additional need, for example, to have the body of the deceased sent back to the village.

When Lulu Waki, a man from the Asaro–Watabung area of the Eastern Highlands, died in Port Moresby, the settlement of Two-Mile was the venue for his death payment. A number of Asaro people in Port Moresby live in a major ethnic sub-section of the settlement, but others who lived in the resettlement area near the university (where the deceased lived and worked), the university barracks and several other parts of town came together at Two-Mile where they contributed the money to send Lulu's body, his wife and children, and a representative of the local community in Port Moresby, back to his village along with a substantial amount of cash to be presented to Lulu's clan. They also collected the money to provide for a funeral feast at Two-Mile itself, later on, for all the contributors (Levine 1976).

Obviously, the settlements with their great density of individuals with close compatriot and kinship ties are natural foci for the networks of primary social relationships which (as we have emphasized before) are necessary to the personal security of urbanites. Perhaps it would be useful at this point to compare the settlements with some of the other types of residential neighbourhoods in the town.

Low-covenant housing estates

Low-covenant houses are usually assigned bureaucratically and arbitrarily so that the residents (typically public servants) have no control over who their neighbours will be. While a settlement dweller is generally surrounded by kin, the low-covenant housing dweller's neighbours may all come from different parts of the country. Nevertheless, traditional ties continue to be important.

Ryan says that the same village-based kinship ties, along which Vabukori formed and is organized, continue to link the settlement dwellers with those Toaripi-speakers who have moved to the low-covenant housing estates. They continue to be part of a network of close personal relationships, reciprocal obligations and shared goods and services (1968: 62).

A study of women living in Hohola housing estate in Port Moresby revealed that every woman kept some rurally oriented ties (i.e. relationships with people who spoke the same vernacular). Most of the women and nearly all of their husbands maintained some sort of land rights in their villages and nearly every couple planned to retire to the husband's or wife's natal home at the end of their working life in the town (Oeser 1969: 34, 47–9, 87).

Residents would regularly return to their villages to attend important traditional celebrations. If they did not do so for a particular occasion, e.g. a funeral feast, one might be held in the housing estate for someone who died in the village. This would be attended solely by members of the same ethnic group. While probably similar in nature to the sorts of events we mentioned occurring in urban settlements, these could hardly be on the same scale (due to limitations of space, if nothing else) (ibid.: 49).

Certain celebrations would, however, be attended by friends and acquaintances who did not belong to the same ethnic group as their hosts. These were usually occasions such as children's birthdays, or going-away parties for children off to school or families departing to holiday in their home village: all non-traditional types of celebrations (ibid.: 40).

Most of the group activity was found to go on in informal local organizations which cropped up spontaneously among the residents: rotating credit associations, card-playing groups and basketball clubs. These tended to be mono-ethnic rather than multi-ethnic.

Formal multi-ethnic associations were occasionally organized, usually by Europeans connected with the government or churches. We will discuss these at greater length in the next chapter, but it is interesting to note that Oeser says that no organization or group could be said to have in any way united the Hohola residents as a whole. She also points out that there was no group or mechanism for neighbourhood dispute settlement (except for the welfare officer or the District Office) and no real community leaders (ibid.: 40–1, 60–3).

Barracks

According to M. Strathern, it is only in the labour compounds that her Hagen informants in Port Moresby lived in close proximity to non-Hageners (1975: 201). Rew, in his study of the barracks housing the employees of a company in Port Moresby, describes how unskilled labourers from eight different New Guinea Highlands and Papuan provinces were assigned quarters in a single house. The most striking aspect of the men's adaptation to their living arrangements is that they grouped their sleeping areas in such a way that the migrants from different parts of the country staked out parts of the house as their own. Furthermore, the daily activities of the men were organized in terms of these groupings. As far as the timing of their shifts allowed, they would cook and eat their food together. After work they might walk to the native market to promenade, meet and talk to friends and kin, etc. This was a largely social expedition as the men seldom bought much in the way of food at the market, mainly sticking to a cheaper, more easily prepared diet of tinned fish and rice.

The existence of such cliques can make life particularly lonely and inconvenient for the occasional labourer who does not fit into any of the groupings. Rew sympathetically describes the situation of the only Morobe man in the barracks. He complained of the exclusive behaviour of the other labourers and, until he left, led a generally miserable existence with no one to eat or cook with, and not even anyone to borrow utensils from.

But this sticking together with co-ethnics, or *wantok*, provides more than convenience and companionship for the townsmen who live in the barracks. There is clearly an element of distrust in the men's attitudes towards labourers from other parts of the country. When thefts occur around the quarters, and when men from different groups become involved in bar brawls, these are discussed by the residents as the inevitable outcome of allowing oneself to be placed in a vulnerable position vis-à-vis people who are not one's *wantok*. Futhermore, it is felt that a man can count only on *wantok* to actively protect him in such a situation.

The relationships of these men living together are, however, of a temporary nature, largely because of the typical instability of unskilled labourers' careers. But the workers also tend to have important relationships with people outside the barracks. This is reflected in the tendency for the number of residents in the barracks (usually about 57) to rise sharply over the weekend. Any sort of housing in the town is a valuable resource and even the meagre accommodation and hospitality that a resident of the barracks is able to offer is not scorned (Rew 1974: 91–135).

In the barracks studied by Rew, the senior indigenous staff (young and skilled) lived in a separate house which was luxurious compared to the barracks. It had running water, electricity, shower, toilet and kitchen facilities. Nevertheless, the problems apparent in the unskilled workers' barracks pertained here as well. Rew provides a rare, detailed account of their situation (ibid.: 45–89) and some of the incidents he records may serve to illustrate the points we have brought out in this section.

The four-bedroomed house had nine staff members (plus Rew) officially living there, who were occasionally outnumbered by their unofficial guests. At any one time there seem to have been at least thirteen or fourteen people in residence, sharing one toilet, shower and table, with two or three making their beds in the common messing area. The overcrowding and resultant squalor became serious sources of contention among the housemates.

The two senior residents, Vincent and John, both Papuans, each had private bedrooms. James (22), a clerk from a Mekeo village in the Central District of Papua, made do with a stretcher set up in the messing area, as did another clerk, Sydney, one of only three New Guineans in the house. The third bedroom was shared by two shift supervisors, Patrick (22) and Bava (20), both Papuans and rather good friends – a rarity in this house where most encounters were characterized by a 'marked reserve and anonymity', and 'a carefully maintained lack of interest in the other residents and their activities' (ibid.: 52).

To the fourth bedroom management assigned Lucian (18), a New Guinean from the Morobe district, and Gabriel (17), a Papuan from James's home village. (Gabriel and James were the only residents who happened to know each other before coming to work for the company.) Although Lucian and Gabriel were of similar age and educational background, and both were metal-trades apprentices in the same workshop, the two were poles apart as individuals. Dividing them on another level were the 'differences in cultural loyalty and identity' inherent in the socially and emotionally potent distinction between Papuan and New Guinean. 'Gabriel and Lucian (Papuan and New Guinean, respectively) were able to express and maintain their differences through their separate identifications with this opposition' (ibid.: 53). Open hostility did not develop, however, until three young men from Gabriel's village moved into the room to sleep on the floor.

One was a boy, Aite, who was finishing his schooling in Port Moresby; he was a dependent kinsman of James, but as an unofficial resident could not stay in the semi-public messing area where James slept. The other two were young men who asked James and Gabriel for a place to sleep until a job or alternative housing turned up. Lucian put up with the noise and untidiness of his three extra room-mates for a few weeks, but finally complained to management that sleep and study were now impossible. When the full extent of the 'unofficial guest' situation emerged, a general (but entirely ineffective) purge was implemented; no one left the house, but Gabriel and the three Mekeo guests moved in with Patrick and Bava, while a third New Guinean staff member (David, who had been staying with relatives in town) moved in with Lucian.

Discord continued, however; it was occasioned by disappearances of food from private cupboards, but mostly centred around the filth and litter that accumulated in the house. Although some residents maintained an unconcerned or philosophical silence, the New Guineans tended to mutter about the inconsiderate Papuans and their guests. For his part James would occasionally press the other Mekeos to help him clean up, all the while grumbling that the New Guineans did not lend a hand.

In effect there was no co-operation nor cohesion as the residents had no time for each other and were completely uninvolved in each others' activities. James, for example, belonged to a Mekeo sports club, was heavily involved with a village business group, and took commercial courses by correspondence. Not only did his affairs leave him little time for his house-mates, but James and his quarters became a centre of attraction for members of both his groups, and their frequent gatherings became yet another burden on the already strained facilities.

James was typical in that, for nearly all the residents, their most important relationships were with kin and co-ethnics living in town, whether their contacts with them were of an organized nature or just casual visiting. The norm in the house was to withdraw when other residents' guests were about, and (except where some two or three had become friendly) they would not even eat with each other, preferring to eat in their bedrooms, or standing up in the kitchen if any of the chairs around the dining table were occupied.

Rew defines a number of elements that served to divide the co-residents, the most salient being that their real interests and significant relationships all lay outside the house. In addition, suggests Rew, their racial attitudes and self-perceptions also held them apart. James, for example, took great pride in his education and 'civilized' ways. His good relations with the expatriates in his office were important to him, he admired Europeans in general, and he always wore the standard white collar uniform of white shirt, tailored shorts, long socks and shoes. Gabriel, by contrast, cultivated a much more rugged style, dressed casually, expressed violent anti-white sentiments upon occasion, and sneered at James's attempts to organize housekeeping, saying that he must have been reprimanded by a European and was afraid of losing his pay. John, although he was at least as concerned as James with projecting himself as an educated and civilized person, was at the same time openly critical of Australian treatment of native people. His articulate denunciations were much appreciated by Gabriel and the younger Papuans, and may thus have undercut James's bids for leadership.

We have already mentioned the part that ethnic identification played in the situation of Lucian and Gabriel. Language, a related factor, set another barrier between the residents, as amongst themselves the three New Guineans would speak pidgin, of which the Papuans had only the most rudimentary grasp. The Papuans would speak in vernacular to their guests, and in Motu to any other Papuans they were friendly with. English was reserved for more formal communication, and indeed most of the speech between house-mates was in that language.

The fact that these young men worked for the same company and that they were lumped together by the management was regarded as merely accidental and not as important as the personal interests, attitudes and indentifications that divided them. On the other hand, these factors did lead to the development of some lower-level ties, that were expressed in eating together and other exchanges, most typically within an ethnic frame of reference. Similar developments were observed in the labourers' barracks where cliques (based on the wider-than-rural extension of kin terms, locality and emergent ethnic loyalties) regarded each other, as we have described previously, with mutual 'suspicion and relatively normless antagonism' (ibid.: 89). When we imagine this situation multiplied many times, in other barracks, and (on a larger scale) in other neighbourhoods as well, we can begin to comprehend the segmented and 'hollow' nature of the town as a whole.

Maintaining communities

Insofar as towns are full of strangers, they are inherently insecure places for Papua New Guineans. In urban settlements, however, relatively secure niches have been created where people are surrounded by kin and co-ethnics. In the low-covenant housing estates the urbanite strives to maintain ties with relatives and *wantok* in the town. The barracks dweller tries as much as possible to isolate himself from the labourers from other parts of the country.

It is impossible, however, for problems with neighbours to be entirely avoided. One of the difficulties of living in low-covenant housing estates and barracks is the lack (already mentioned) of mechanisms for cross-ethnic dispute settlement. But problems arise between co-ethnics as well, particularly in situations where members of enemy clans live in the same settlement. For example, an Asaro informant living in Two-Mile settlement in Port Moresby told us that parents regularly warned their children not to accept food from certain households in the settlement for fear that someone might try to even an old clan score through the use of sorcery or poison (Levine 1976).

Dispute settlement mechanisms within *wantok* groups vary quite a bit. According to M. Strathern, the fact that no big-men have migrated to Port Moresby to become part of the urban Hagen community leads to serious problems of social control, since there is no one sufficiently endowed with the oratorical technique, the ability to manage people, and social prestige necessary to settle disputes effectively (1975: 376). But in the Asaro–Watabung community of Two-Mile settlement we witnessed the consummate skill with which certain men (who were big-men in their villages and highly respected leaders of the settlement community, despite being uneducated, unemployed and perennially dependent) could mould the opinions and feelings of their fellow townsmen with their finely argued analyses of current disputes. What seemed like an explosive and potentially community-shattering situation (resulting from a trivially inspired but rather ugly drunken fight) was soon resolved in a scene of reconciliation and, of course, compensation (Levine 1976).

A much more commonplace aspect of the problem of mutual dependence that every urbanite has is that of keeping up these primary social ties. They must be continually cultivated in the town even if they had a pre-existing rural base. One of the ways in which the townsmen maintain networks of social relationships and provide security for each other is by taking *pasendia* (passengers) and visitors from their villages into their homes in the town. Some low-covenant housing dwellers and most people who live in barracks are severely limited in the degree to which they can do this if their quarters are supplied by an employer who enforces restrictions on who may live with them. But in the urban settlements (and where there are no such restrictions) people will nearly always feel obliged to take in a migrant who can claim some kin or compatriot tie and is new to the town. People who have nowhere to live, either because they have lost a job or had a falling-out with former co-residents, are also taken in. This attitude is a very adaptive one as anyone who extends hospitality can expect to find their generosity returned. M. Strathern suggests that there are limits to this among Hageners living in Port Moresby; while the new migrant will always be taken in, a *pasendia* who remains idle for too long is criticized and may wear out his welcome, especially if it is felt that he is not trying hard enough to find work. Furthermore, a smart host will want to make the most of his resources in terms of helping many of his *wantok*, rather than committing himself to the long-term support of just one (1975: 61–2).

Visitors from home can be an even greater drain on a household, yet one which tends to be entirely accepted. They are the most important tie that migrants have with their relatives back home. Migrants sometimes count on visitors to relay messages and gifts. Townsmen who have intentions of returning to their villages are particularly likely to go out of their way for visitors, and to keep home ties alive against the time they finally do return and can call on their favours to be reciprocated. This may commonly come in the form of aid in amassing brideprice, for example.

Whiteman, in her study of Chimbu in Port Moresby, suggests that in addition to norms of reciprocal obligation and the expectation that favours will eventually be returned, there is a strong fear that witchcraft will be used against those who do not help fellow townsmen or visitors. This is said to result in misfortune or the illness and death of children or other members of the immediate family of the stingy party (1973: 129). Oeser's Papuan informants expressed similar fears (1969: 75–6).

Whatever the reasons, visitors from home tend to be treated with extraordinary generosity. In the Badili canoe settlement, visitors from Hula were given substantial cash gifts on their departure by their hosts (Oram 1967: 30–1). Oeser mentions that her informants' food and drink expenditures were more closely related to the presence of visitors than to the size of the family, suggesting that they were very elaborately wined and dined (1969: 75). M. Strathern says that not only are Hagen visitors presented with air-tickets back home and large cash gifts by their hosts and close relatives in the town, but other Hagen townsmen will present the returning visitors with money as well. She feels that this provides an opportunity for them to express solidarity by helping out with the send-off of a fellow migrant's relative (1975: 346–62).

In addition, the visitors expect to be shown a good time while they are in town and to see the sights of the city. Some old Asaro men (from the Eastern Highlands Province) said that they came down to Port

Moresby for the express purpose of seeing the *solwara* (ocean) before they died. But probably the most common way of entertaining visitors is taking them to the bars in the town and drinking with them. A Papuan informant told us about the time her husband's cousin came to visit. He felt obliged to take the man drinking every night, even though he himself did not ordinarily frequent the bars. Informants from the Eastern Highlands claimed that certain Port Moresby drinking spots were famous back home and that every visitor had to be taken to them (Levine 1976).

The towns' bars are not merely places to entertain visitors, however, and neither is it coincidental that they have become urban landmarks. Even though drinking can by no means be called a universal activity (some urbanites have strong religious scruples against the practice) it can certainly be said to be an important form of recreation for urban men in general. Beyond recreation, drinking is one of the activities that men can indulge in together, expressing their fellow-feeling in buying drinks for each other.

On the other hand, it can just as easily lead to fights and is widely regarded as a major urban social problem. Wives complain that they can hardly feed their families because their husbands may drink away their entire pay packet, while some men say they make a point of rendering up the bulk of their pay to their wives to avoid just such a calamity. In Mount Hagen, enmity between Hagens and Wabags is commonly traced back to major bar brawls between urbanites from the two areas.

Some Buang men claimed that the reason they migrated to Lae in the first place was so that they could get drunk regularly. According to Zimmerman, her informants would drink to express their masculinity, their drinking ability, wealth (lining up the empty glasses on the table) and prestige. Drinking also tended to lead to both intra- and inter-village fights among the urbanites (1973: 90). One of her informants said that Buangs only drank with other Buangs, and certainly it is part of the conventional wisdom of townspeople that this is the wisest policy. The prevalence of inter-ethnic bar brawls attest, however, to the difficulty of avoiding other ethnics in bars. Undoubtedly though, helping out a clansman or *wantok* in such a fight provides the townsmen with an expression and consolidation of the sorts of social relationships that ensure him a measure of personal security in the town.

Gambling (card-playing) is another popular activity which tends to be taken fairly seriously by the migrants. Occasionally it functions to redistribute cash resources through the community (at least for those who play together regularly). Some townsmen see gambling as a source of income potentially far greater than their wages. It is also an activity that often brings together people from different parts of the country, particularly if they work together or live in different sections of the same multi-ethnic settlement or the same low-covenant housing estate. The groups will then play cards against each other in teams.

Other common recreational activities include sports, attending the cinema, picnics (almost always within groups of kin since most townspeople would feel insecure in an isolated part of the countryside, eating and drinking with people that they could not entirely trust) (M. Strathern 1975: 225), casual visiting (for a meal or to spend a few nights) and informal religious services or prayer meetings in peoples' homes in the evening.

Townsmen also depend upon each other for straightforward financial support in terms of loans and informal rotating credit associations, where they regularly (weekly or fortnightly) pool some portion of their wages which is given to the members in turn. This allows the individuals to make occasional major investments in a situation where regular savings are subject to the depredations of needy kin and salaries are very low to begin with. It is interesting to note that this is another activity that may bring together urbanites from different parts of the country.

Women in the local community

Since women are (as we shall see) less likely to move out of the urban residential domain than men, their social lives are most fundamentally centred around specific housing areas. For this reason women's roles, relationships and activities may be appropriately examined within the context of a discussion of local neighbourhoods.

Any discussion of women in Papua New Guinean towns suffers from the lack of breadth of the available data. While it has been possible to study certain specific groups and categories of women, some fieldworkers have described the difficulties involved in including them in their research.

M. Strathern, in the course of her study of Hagen migrants to Port Moresby, makes penetrating and valuable comments about the lives of female migrants but points out that there are very few Hagen women in the town. Whiteman's study of Chimbu family relations in the urban environment also deals with a very small sample of women. Oeser's intensive study of thirteen women residents in Hohola housing estate is quite useful but obviously limited in scope.

Zimmerman, on the other hand, flatly states that she could not talk to the Buang women living in Lae (1973: 88). In our own efforts to include a cross-section of women in a survey of townspeople in Mount Hagen and Port Moresby, we experienced considerable difficulty, particularly in trying to interview the largely uneducated and unemployed women living in the urban settlements. The problem was less their reticence than the insistence of local men that the women could not possibly be of enough significance or have anything of enough interest to say to warrant a European interviewer wasting his or her time on them. The obvious implication that they (the men) would be pleased to chat and answer questions instead made it difficult to insist on speaking to the women. (Male Papua New Guinean research assistants were somewhat more successful than we were but the female research assistants, whom we thought would be the real answer to this problem, felt harassed by male settlement dwellers and too uncomfortable to continue interviewing.)

This insignificance attributed to migrant women by local men is actually a key to their urban position. Unlike some of their African counterparts, Papua New Guinean townswomen have not yet developed a place for themselves on the urban scene. While a number of individuals have achieved a certain prominence (Oram 1967: 147), most female urbanites find their positions to be marginal and their status diminished in the towns. Although one of the present government's stated priorities is the advancement of equality of opportunity for women (Somare 1975: 109), they are in the meantime not as well educated as male urbanites, far less likely to be employed and less prestigiously so. They also tend to speak fewer languages and have much less contact with members of other ethnic groups.

Any woman who moves to town loses (for most intents and purposes) the roles and relationships she had in the village. If she is largely confined to the urban settlement her husband resides in, then she is unlikely to replace those relationships on a very significant scale. For many women urban life is very limiting. Whether they live in the urban settlements, low-covenant housing estates or married quarters, their activities are confined to minor housekeeping, collecting firewood and maybe gathering shellfish, looking after infants and doing a limited amount of gardening if they are lucky enough to live in a town where some arable land is available to them.

Oeser found a great deal of variation in the actual size of the urban social networks of thirteen women living in Hohola low-covenant housing estate. The women varied in the number of 'traditional' relationships they maintained (i.e. with people who spoke the same vernacular) and in the number of 'urban' associations (people who did not speak their vernacular). She found that the urban associations did *not* tend to replace the traditional ones and that the women who seemed best adjusted to urban life had larger numbers of both (1969: 32–6). However, all of these women were coastal Papuans. Although their position in the town in terms of options and status was about as limited as that of the rest of the female population, they tended to be more familiar with the urban environment as their people had had a longer history of contact, and they had a larger population of co-ethnics living in the town.

For Highlands women the contrast with village life may be the strongest. At home they are the breadwinners of the family. They are entirely responsible for feeding themselves and their children (and sometimes their husbands) from the vegetable gardens and for raising pigs which are major traditional wealth items. Furthermore, M. Strathern points out that Hagen women in town lose their rural importance as social intermediaries, since personal friendship networks assume greater importance than traditional webs of affinity. Ryan (1970: 81), M. Strathern (1975) and Levine (1976) suggest that although rurally based kin and affinal ties are very important in providing *potential* social network links, they must be activated and maintained by individual actions in the town. Thus, a Hagen woman's independence is further circumscribed by the fact that her only social outlet, according to Strathern, is card-playing. If this is 'one of the few activities in which both sexes mix and interact freely' (M. Strathern 1975: 222), then clearly a woman is limited in the range of social relationships she can cultivate.

The importance of gambling is stressed by a number of fieldworkers (Oeser 1969: 62, Whiteman 1973: 53) and for women it is particularly important as a source of entertainment and potential income. It is a spectator sport for any woman lacking a stake, while others claim to feed their families and contribute significant amounts of cash for other purchases and gift-giving from their winnings.

But however much some women may win at cards, female urbanites are by-and-large economically dependent on their menfolk. As Oeser points out, this is a new kind of power for Papua New Guinea's men and a new kind of dependence for the women (1969: 80). For a number of reasons there may be a tendency for men to supply their wives with less money than they really need to feed the family properly. The vast majority of urban men are unskilled and may not make very much money to begin with. Many find it difficult to accept or adjust to the way in which the town 'eats' their pay. In the village one can feed, clothe and shelter a family without necessarily spending any cash at all. In keeping up their networks of urban social relationships men may have many demands made on their slender wages, in terms of loans to *wantok*, investments in various enterprises such as rural trade stores or a truck in the town, such expressions of personal generosity and friendship as buying drinks in the bar, and of course the gifts that are given to visitors or sent to the village. At the same time, women are often called upon not only to provide food for their immediate family but to feed other household members (often young males, related to themselves or to their husbands, who may or may not be employed or contributing to the food budget), casual guests and visitors to the town. In addition, they may feel that they must send gifts to their own village and kin, again fearing sorcery if they do not fulfil expectations (as well as having more altruistic motives). Judicious gift giving is also thought to be necessary to prevent dangerous jealousy on the part of their kin, and this, coupled with the financial demands mentioned above, means that the urban housewife's slender budget may be severely taxed.

Whiteman records the response of the house-guests of one of her informants when she asked them why they did not give their host any money to defray the costs of putting them up. They said, 'In Chimbu when we go to stay with people we don't pay rent or provide food' (1973: 61). M. Strathern, on the other hand, says that Hagen migrants feel obliged to give Hagen women (if they are living in the town and are dependent on their husbands) occasional gifts of a few dollars. She suggests that women who do the best they can with the demands made on their hospitality gain a certain amount of leverage over their husbands and guests, whereas those making direct demands on their husbands tend to be resented by other Hageners who may not see such claims as being any more valid than their own (1975: 214).

This extreme economic dependency of Papua New Guinean towns-women may be largely due to the recency of their presence in urban centres. Certainly the situation for women in towns in sub-Saharan Africa (where the urbanization process is similar though further developed) is markedly different. The first women to move into African towns were usually (as in Papua New Guinea) joining their already-established hus-bands, but soon the spectrum of migrating females widened to include single, divorced and widowed women with dependent children. All of these women expected to find opportunities for making money, despite the fact that they, too, are not as well educated as the men. In many parts of Africa (both areas with and without a tradition of female traders), townswomen dominate the market-places and petty trading in general, in addition to owning shops, beer-halls, etc. They often set up their own urban voluntary organizations for the purpose of facilitating and regulating trade, promoting solidarity and arbitrating disputes. Even prostitutes will sometimes form protective associations rather than relying on pimps (Little 1973).

Thus, instead of becoming more dependent many African women achieve a substantial degree of independence in town. But in Papua New Guinea, as things stand now, few women are employed or in business, and even prostitution is on a relatively small scale and casually organized (Oram 1976: 163). However, those Papua New Guinean women who are employed tend to have control over their own incomes (even when they are married) and contribute to household expenditures on a voluntary basis.

Making a place for themselves in the towns will probably involve Papua New Guinean women in more than just finding jobs and making money, as the sorts of wider functions that African women's urban voluntary associations have taken on are essential to an independent option for urban women. These organizations assist female migrants in adjusting to city life by teaching them social skills and western ways, helping them towards professions, providing formal care for visitors and new arrivals and teaching them to orient themselves to the class system. They also provide a new urban reference group which furnishes companionship to replace village relationships and power to advance women's interests. The improvement of Papua New Guinean women's position in the towns may well depend on the emergence of such effective associations in the future.

But employment, the wider urban field in general and the development of urban voluntary associations in Papua New Guinea are topics that we take up in later chapters. For now, having discussed in some detail the contexts in which urbanites enter into close personal relationships, we will turn to an analysis of the idioms and principles involved in the formation of those ties.

Some urban social categories

Entering into primary relationships is facilitated by certain modes of classifying people in the urban environment. We certainly would not, at this point in our discussion, expect a local person to attempt to establish a primary relationship with just anybody. In all societies and social situations people classify each other in a variety of ways which are instrumental in influencing social interaction. By focusing on any number of culturally relevant characteristics, people may approach others with certain expectations of how a relationship should develop and proceed. In Papua New Guinean towns three discernible principles of social categorization – kinship, friendship and ethnicity – serve as important idioms of primary relationship which orient people towards certain individuals and away from others. Each of these modes of classifying other urbanites carries sets of defining principles (to determine who to include or exclude as a member) and notions of rights and obligations that imply a (sometimes vague) moral bond between those falling within the category. It should be stressed that the categories themselves provide for potential, not certain, relationships. In each case particular sequences of strategies involving the use of transactions are necessary to create an actual relationship out of a potential one. Transactions (the patterned transference of material and immaterial items between individuals) also provide a mechanism whereby individuals with no prior expectations of a

relationship may come to form one. Since kinship, friendship and ethnicity are ubiquitous idioms of social relationship involving all urban Papua
New Guineans in a series of personal networks, cliques, coalitions and
groups, understanding their principles of definition and operation allows
us to gain insight into the kind of everyday social relationships which
develop in the towns. In addition to considering how these primary
relationships form it is also necessary to note the ways in which the
patterns of association they generate may differ from rural groupings.
This allows for an appreciation of the way in which local urban
environments influence the development of distinctive forms of social
relationship.

Kinship, friendship and ethnicity: preliminary considerations

When discussing social categories we should distinguish between those
which social scientists use to describe and analyse behaviour and those
used by our informants. In the case of kinship there would be relatively
little disparity between a Melanesian and anthropological definition. The
term refers to culturally specific ideas and methods of categorizing people
in terms of real or putative ties of consanguinity and affinity. When an
urban Papua New Guinean enters into a relationship with someone whom
he reckons 'shares blood' or is tied to him through marriage, defining that
relationship as having a kinship base is usually a fairly straightforward
matter.

Ethnicity is another basis of relationship which is fairly unambiguous as
both a native and observer category. In urban Papua New Guinea people
often interact with reference to subjective beliefs in common origin (a
definition of ethnicity which follows from Weber (1961)) which are based
on hailing from the same place. As will be discussed further below, 'same
place' may be used to designate broad or specific areas depending on the
social situation in which ethnic claims are made. The Papua New Guinean
emphasis on 'place' is interesting in light of the fact that many anthropological and sociological definitions of ethnicity start with an
assumption that culture provides its basic frame of reference. As one
might expect, peoples of similar culture do tend to live together, so
cultural similarity (itself a very relative concept) is partially accounted for
in terms of this geographic reference. However, urban Papua New Guineans do not emphasize considerations of custom. When discussing participants in relationships and events who are defined with reference to
subjective beliefs in common origin, local townsmen use an expandable
spatial referent.

In the case of friendship it is a bit more difficult to reconcile western and
Papua New Guinean definitions closely. Certainly, ease of interaction and
a willingness to spend free time together are typical of friendly relations

everywhere. But Papua New Guineans are less likely than westerners to exclude kinsmen from a list of 'friends'. For example, a term commonly glossed as friend, *wantok*, is used by local people in reference to all primary relationships regardless of principle of recruitment. Examining the meaning and use of this Papua New Guinean urban social category will enable us to gain considerable insight into the formation of local primary relationships and the connection between urban kinship, friendship, ethnicity and transactions. But since kinship is an important pre-urban framework of social categorization we will begin with a consideration of its use in local towns.

Kinship in urban Papua New Guinea

The basic organizing principle in small-scale societies all over the world is kinship. In rural areas of Papua New Guinea kinship systems commonly define and regulate membership in most important groups. Land rights and access to other necessary resources, exchange relationships, political arenas, possible marriage partners and patterns of alliance and enmity are all aspects of village life in which kinship plays a fundamental role. Since virtually all urban Papua New Guinean adults have been brought up in villages it is not surprising that kinship provides an essential pre-existing basis for urban social relationships. As was mentioned in our discussion of migration, people from rural areas commonly migrate to towns which contain close relatives. These people usually take newcomers in, introduce them to urban ways, help in job-hunting, etc. The great deal of circulation between town and village also reinforces the relevance of home ties in town. But kinship in urban areas is often not the same phenomenon that it is in the villages.[1] Access to the requisites of life in towns, such as money, jobs and housing, is not controlled by kinship groups. Also, the preponderance of young single males in the urban population and the fact that kinsmen who do migrate are often scattered in various towns (and/or in different residential areas of the same town)

[1] The reader might be interested in making comparisons between the conclusions developed in this section and those come to about other towns in other areas. In a rather general volume dealing with Third World urbanization, Gutkind maintains that 'only truncated segments of kin units are found in the urban community' because the conditions commensurate with kinship are not often present in post-colonial towns (1974: 156). Little (1974: 24) feels that urbanization usually involves the replacement of communalistic patterns by individualistic ones. Other authors stress the continuity between rural and urban kinship. Bruner states that Toba Batak lineages remain corporate in Medan, Indonesia (1963). Many other studies (e.g. Mayer (1961) on the Xhosa of East London) refer to the use of rural idioms such as kinship in urban life. Even in situations of the greatest continuity, however, it is important to examine the specific urban conditions which permit this.

make it unlikely that a sufficient range of personnel exists to enable migrants to re-create rural kin groups in urban areas. This lack of personnel and resource-base varies for different groups in the urban areas. As we shall see in this section, certain rural functions of kinship (its use as an element in political organization or in the allocation of land rights, for example) are only rarely carried over into towns. As a basis of domestic organization or an idiom of social relationships, however, more continuity may be noted. But even under these circumstances we must stress that kinship is more than just a rural import. It becomes a key element in the formation of distinctively urban relationships as the solidarity of kinsmen and the use of kinship idioms are fundamentally affected by a constellation of factors involved with the urbanization process. These ensure that a rural basis of relationship will produce distinctive social forms in urban areas.

A number of the studies cited earlier in this chapter have addressed the question of urban kinship and allow us to appreciate the ways in which kin ties are used and the sorts of urban relationships which develop out of them in Papua New Guinea.

The Toaripi in Port Moresby (Ryan 1968, 1970) quite successfully organize many of their activities along rural village lines, and provide an example of great continuity of corporate group and interpersonal kinship organization in town. The landholding system in Vabukori settlement, regulating the formation of housing clusters, is based on traditional kinship principles. People share food, money and housing in ways much like those of village areas, and in the course of everyday life refer back to kin ties and principles operative at home. Ryan says that Moresby's Toaripi have re-created a village environment in the town fairly successfully (1968: 62). This is probably due to the fact that a large number of these Gulf Province people have left home, the great majority with their families. Most urban Toaripi (3000 out of 3300 at the time of the study) live in Port Moresby where they have been able to acquire urban land through past relationships with Motu and Koita right-holders. They are long-term (stable) urban residents and fairly concentrated in the building trades. Port Moresby's proximity to their home area permits a ready flow of messages and people between town and village which further strengthens the role of rural affairs in urban life.

Urban villagers (people whose villages are located in or near the boundary of an urban centre) are obviously in an ideal position to use kinship as a resource in relation to the urban environment. Epstein (1969), discussing social change in the Tolai area around Rabaul town, stresses the continuity and flexibility of local traditions in peri-urban villages there.

But along with this continuity for urban villagers there is great change.

Port Moresby's Motu and Koita *iduhu* (clans) have lost many of their old corporate group functions as gardening and fishing have been replaced by wage-labour. Leaders of local kin groups (where they are known) have little authority and marriages are contracted by a less extensive group of kin than before. Nevertheless, *iduhu* members retain a certain sense of corporate identity, and clan membership is important in relation to church affairs (Epstein 1969: 134, Oram 1976: 134). Although both Moresby's *iduhu* and Tolai *vunatari* remain important social units, it seems clear that present Tolai kinship groups are considerably more durable than Motu and Koita ones (Epstein 1969: 317–18). This difference is a direct result of urban and peri-urban development. Port Moresby is large enough to absorb most of its autochthonous inhabitants as wage-labourers. These people are involved in more sectors of the urban economy than are workers of most other groups. Gardening is fairly difficult in the capital's dry environment and was abandoned as a means of subsistence some time ago (Belshaw 1957). When the Motu and Koita villagers became more involved with the greatly expanding city of Port Moresby as workers, the *iduhu* lost some of its *raison d'être*. In the Tolai area, on the other hand, villagers vastly outnumber townsmen. Although the Tolai are among the most dynamic businessmen in Papua New Guinea, their enterprises centre on cash-crops. Tolai workers in Rabaul (which can absorb only a limited number of them) keep a vital interest in their productive land, access to which is controlled by kinship groups.

As these examples show, kinship can be used as the basis for urban group and property organization in certain circumstances. People living in towns close to their home area, who can localize residence in the urban environment (in urban villages or settlements), have their families and sufficient other kin with them, and are concentrated in discrete sectors of the urban economy, may be able to transpose rural (or maintain local) kinship forms in towns with some success, using them for a great variety of purposes. But for many urbanites, even where a number of these factors are present (e.g. the Motu–Koita case), circumstances mitigate against the formation of multi-purpose corporate urban kinship groupings.

The Toaripi in Lae, for example, provide an interesting contrast to those in Port Moresby. The move to that town, inaccessible to the Gulf Province except by a prohibitively expensive air service, has resulted in decreased contact with the home area in terms of both visits and letter-writing. People in Lae are neither consulted nor asked to participate in village kin group activities and hold no festivals to coincide with village ones as do the Toaripi in Port Moresby. Because the 300 Toaripi in Lae are employed in relatively well-paid positions (whereas 20 per cent of Moresby's Toaripi are unemployed) there is little need for kin to help one another financially. The smallness of the Toaripi population and the mix of people of different rural kin units present in Lae means that relatively few people are bound by close pre-existing kin ties. The housing situation is so difficult in Lae that local Toaripi find it impossible to offer space to any but close relatives. Ryan states that these urbanites have been lost to the village and in Lae there has been no re-creation of Toaripi village life (1968: 64). Other researchers have also noted the diminished importance of corporate kin groups for people in towns far from their home area (Bedford and Mamak 1976, Levine 1976, Oram 1976, M. Strathern 1975, Whiteman 1973).

Of course, although kin groups identical or similar to village units may not often develop in Papua New Guinea's towns, it does not follow that kinship or kinship idioms are not important for all indigenous urban Papua New Guineans. In fact, when kinship is *not* used to form groups it often has more interesting implifications for urban social organization than when it *is* so used.

Individuals may, for example, use their various personal kinship connections instrumentally or eclectically, drawing on ties in urban areas that would not commonly be the basis of interaction in the country. While most rural societies in Papua New Guinea have a unilineal (often patrilineal) ideology, ties of matrifiliation and marriage (which may occasionally facilitate recruitment to groups in rural areas) are, of course, recognized. Nevertheless, unilineality remains the ideal basis for group formation in most village areas. But in towns where corporate kin groups are typically absent, a great range of kin may be approached for occasional favours or companionship. At the same time, only a narrow clique of close relatives are usually willing to provide sustained financial assistance, to see a needy townsman through an initial adjustment period or times of unemployment (Oram 1967, Seifert 1975: 105, M. Strathern 1975: 105). This is rather to be expected in a situation where money, not clan land, is a vital resource and not often earned through group effort. This expansion and contraction of kin referents to fit situational urban needs makes urban kinship more of an individual strategy than a group-formation mechanism.

While investigating Chimbu family relationships in Port Moresby, Whiteman (1973) noted that no common boundaries of kin relationships existed for those families she studied. Often a small group of men would arrive at a house and their hosts would have no blood or affinal connection with them. 'They only knew that they were Chimbu and they came to visit them with someone whom they did know' (Whiteman 1973: 93). The complicated (but rather common) situation of distant classificatory, affinal or matrilateral kin of kinsmen and their friends being introduced to a man (who himself may not know or have heard of them previously) is frequently glossed by reference to place, and this facilitates the formation of primary ethnic cliques. Also, kin terms may be used to denote compatriot relationships. Whiteman mentions that in certain situations all Chimbu may regard each other as brothers. In this sense, the kinship term is used to indicate the nature of the relationship and not a genealogical or affinal connection. This is also true where urbanites establish ties with people from different provinces whom they have met in the town, and discuss these relationships in (fictive) kin terms (Oram 1967: 33–4).

In this way, kinship may be instrumental in forming urban ethnic categories, which can precipitate out of situations in which individual networks are mobilized for such affairs as parties, funerals or recreational events. Although we have stressed that corporate groups equivalent to rural ones may often be impossible to re-form, in certain instances people in urban areas do attempt to develop special-purpose groups (analogous to ones which would form at home through the use of rural kinship principles) despite a lack of 'correct' personnel.

An important institution in rural Hagen society is the *moka* system of ceremonial exchange (A. J. Strathern 1971). This is a mechanism of group competition and alliance, and is often instrumental in establishing relative group prestige and peace between warring tribal units at home. Hagen migrants in Port Moresby organize 'parties' which operate in ways similar to the rural *moka* (M. Strathern 1975: 225–40). These involve a formal series of exchanges of food and drink which obligate the recipients to make a larger return in the future. One example reported at length (ibid.: 172–92) involved an attempt to reconcile a serious and violent dispute between some Northern Melpa and Kaugel people (who are both from the Hagen sub-district and able to operate in reference to a common cultural idiom, and sometimes view each other as fellow ethnics in Port Moresby). In organizing for the urban series of presentations the North-ern Melpa men divided themselves into sub-groups according to where they live in town. Instead of rural men's house units they formed into groups of 'Waigani men', 'Six-Mile men', etc., and prepared food and drink for a formal presentation made on the grounds of the Admin-istrative College where a number of Northern Melpa had jobs. In keeping with *moka* custom, the Kaugel presented a return gift which was greater than that given to them. This in turn obligated the Northern Melpa to make an even bigger party in future. In attempting to arrange for this distribution they tried to enlarge their base of support by involving a wide range of other Melpa in the party at which they received food. But these people did not feel obliged to help in the return gift and the expanded Melpa to Kaugel gift exchange fell flat.

The limited success of this urban *moka* was due to the fact that in the urban environment organization proceeded in reference to wider, more tenuously linked, heterogeneous and anonymous units than would have been used at home. In the village area, exact personal knowledge of 'who is to receive what' in the discrete segmentary kin framework of gift giving and receiving is quite possible. Even a bad exchange is not likely to cause rupturing of relations between groups linked by many past and present ties of kinship, exchange, affinity, etc. In Port Moresby, however, a group large enough to make *moka* is extremely heterogeneous by rural standards. As there are insufficient members of small kin groups to do things correctly in Port Moresby, men from many Hagen, Kaugel and Temboka tribes were involved. Although kinship and other rural idioms were operating in this situation, we were again presented with an instance of their use leading to the formation of groups ultimately defined in terms of a geographical unit: in this case, the Mount Hagen sub-district of the Western Highlands Province.

Still other attempts to use kinship idioms have had similar results. Urban Siane (who come from an area near Goroka) seek out older men as contacts for jobs. The focal role of these men derives in part from the emphasis on seniority and importance of older brothers in Siane lineage structure (Salisbury and Salisbury 1970). But in urban work situations the personnel and relationships involved differ for reasons similar to the case described above. True Siane lineages are most unlikely to re-form as work lines, although clusters of 'Gorokas' quite frequently eventuate. A desire to find congenial company has also led Buangs in Port Moresby into closer and more frequent contact with kin from a wider range of villages than in the home area (Zimmerman 1973: 149).

In general, then, kinship is a very important basis for establishing primary relationships, but the urban use of this pre-existing rural social referent only leads to the re-formation of rural types of kin groups in the rather special circumstances discussed above. For most townsmen, a small group of close kin provide the greatest support while other kin are approached on an individual basis. The diminished sense of clanship in towns is replaced by the use of a variety of kin connections and idioms as a fundamental basis of the formation of personal networks. When used in the formation of transitory urban groups or cliques, these often bring together units that essentially become situational urban ethnic groups.

Ethnicity and primary relationships

As we have just seen, the eclectic use of pre-existing kinship relations in urban areas rapidly becomes an element in the development of another principle of primary relations, ethnicity. Much of the literature dealing with ethnicity in urban areas in various parts of the world stresses the functions ethnic units perform for either the individual or the urban social system. Scholars dealing with the local scene have mentioned that ethnic classifications help individuals to order, or make sense of, the great mix of people present in the towns, providing a set of initial expectations for inter-ethnic encounters. Ethnic units are also said to provide reference groups in which migrants find prestige and emotional security (M. Strathern 1975), and categories of self-identification which also form part of their ordering of the urban populations (Rew 1974). As we have stressed previously, ethnicity is one basic system of social categorization that facilitates the formation of primary relationships which help urban Papua New Guineans to establish a base for entering and remaining involved in urban life. All of these functions of ethnicity are quite common to cities everywhere and this has been recognized in the urban anthropological literature at least since Mitchell's seminal work in central Africa (1956).

Knowing the functions of ethnicity helps us to understand the social processes involved in urbanization. However, such discussions are often less helpful in explaining the social construction of urban ethnic units, or why such functions are carried out in an ethnic idiom in the first place, and not with reference to class or neighbourhood, for example. Appreciating the way in which ethnic formations are socially constructed allows us to gain greater insight into how social categories are influenced by and in turn act back upon the urban system.

A specific reason for stressing ethnic construction in urban areas of Papua New Guinea is that ethnicity is the most important framework for the development of extra-kin social relations and the mobilization of wider social units in the towns. By examining how ethnic units form we can understand why they are so multi-functional and have such a central role in the operation of the dialectical social processes forging Papua New Guinean towns out of formerly colonial centres.

A number of ingredients essential to this discussion have been brought forward in earlier chapters. We know that traditional social units in Papua New Guinea were extremely small, isolated, and cumulatively present a picture of great cultural diversity. A common ethnic terminology for all urban dwellers cannot be constructed in reference to such units, each of which may only be known to a small number of people and irrelevant except in very specific micro-level urban interactions. The colonial divisions of the country (specifically, the names of provincial head-quarters) and the wider regions composed of them, do, on the other hand, provide a convenient (expandable) reference for such a terminology, which also fits very well with the pervasive emphasis on 'place' (mentioned above and to be discussed in greater detail in the next section). Due to the pattern of colonial contact, present levels of rural development, and the coincidence of region of origin and socio-economic status in the towns, stereotypes based on dichotomies of 'primitive' and 'civilized' attach to these labels. They also facilitate the naming of cliques formed non-ethnically (as seen in our discussion of the operation of kinship principles) and further encourage the recruitment of others (who are similarly labelled) to these social networks. Once people define their cliques as 'Chimbu', for example, other Chimbu are also *wantok* even if no prior connection to them exists.

The logic of this system of categorization based on province of origin encourages a wider than traditional self-identification. However, this is not the only, nor necessarily the greatest, push in the direction of greater inclusiveness in urban primary groups. Various government services, such as rural development funds, agricultural extension, radio and health services, are organized on a provincial level. Electoral boundaries which regulate competition for these resources are also drawn to coincide with administrative boundaries. People who have gone to a high school or who have met in a town next to their area of origin are likely to be from the same province and, when in a town far away from home, tend to develop a compatriot relationship. The colonial and independent government administrations have both been important in fostering provincial identities (Ballard 1976: 4–6). These become operative in towns as bases of self-identification when wider than rural cliques form.

So far, we have been stressing the role of self-designation in our discussion of ethnic identities. Ascription (definitions by other people) are at least as important in the creation of ethnic units and greatly influence self-identifications. In numerous situations people see aggregations of individuals around the town. They label these aggregations in terms of general ethnic categories. For example, we find that in squatter settlements clusters of houses inhabited by people from a specific group of villages from a very discrete area are often labelled by other residents in very general terms (Levine 1976). Particular Eastern Highlanders (e.g. members of the Kofena phratry from the Asaro–Watabung area, west of Goroka) may label Toaripis as 'Keremas' or 'Papuans' and in turn be designated 'Gorokas' or 'Highlanders'. When used frequently enough between members and by outsiders these labels often stick, especially where the in-group is itself composed of people from the same area who may have known each other at home, but were not part of the same rural social unit. When disputes occur, others to whom the label applies often join in and higher-level ethnic coalitions form. For example, if one of the 'Keremas' assaults a 'Goroka', the relatives of the victim may decide to waylay a 'Kerema' for a payback and wind up thrashing someone totally unrelated to the original culprit. The relatives of this second victim may in return attack a 'Highlander' from another province. Suddenly a mass of Highlanders and Papuans may find themselves (possibly unwilling) disputants. These generalizations, the ignoring of internal distinctions, and the local tendency to hold groups responsible for what westerners might feel are individual matters, produce large-scale ethnic schisms out of small-scale disputes. The ethnic terminological hierarchy guides the labelling of these categories and the perceptions of relative closeness that lead to overtures for primary relationships and mutual aid (ibid.).

One of the more interesting aspects of this phenomenon is that it masks tribal enmities in towns, at least in situations where higher-level disputes are occurring. People who might find themselves shooting at each other at home may, through the eclectic use of kin ties, be neighbours in a settlement. Their rural differences (social or cultural) seem less important in the town than the fact that there are a lot of more obviously alien types about, some of whom may have evil designs. Besides, they may share a water-pipe, can speak about common acquaintances, tip each other off about job vacancies, and have many other things in common. In the circumstances of urban life they may become relatively close and disparage the importance of village politics. At the same time, they often take precautions against sorcery and sneak attacks, just to be on the safe side, especially when rural events reinforce the importance of traditional units (Levine 1976, M. Strathern 1975). The power of these rural events to do so largely depends on how far one is from the home area. Tambul (Kaugel) informants in Mount Hagen, for example, never had anything to do with members of enemy clans. The village was only thirty miles away and fighting always threatened. In Port Moresby these enemies were more willing to consider each other compatriots (along with Melpa speakers who were generally avoided in Hagen town) and engaged in various transactions together.

When we say that urban ethnic units are socially constructed, we do not mean that they are consciously erected or even (on lower levels especially) used as deliberate strategies to gain control of urban resources. Individuals often operate other idioms (e.g. kinship) but find themselves and others referring to the cliques they form in ethnic terms and giving ethnic explanations for their behaviour to those unfamiliar with their specific cultural idiom.

Ethnic units are generated via the processes mentioned (i.e. labelling, self-identification and ascription, schismogenesis (cf. Bateson 1936)), but take their particular form in response to urban events and situations. Not only are the ethnic units urban located, but the very labels involved in their development are a response to both general urban factors (heterogeneity and relative anonymity produced by the migration process, needs of employers, housing shortages, etc.) and specific urban events such as disputes arising in particular work lines, random automobile accidents, brawls, etc. These determine the sorts of conflicts that will arise, whether they are likely to be recurrent, and how inclusive the resulting ethnic units will be.

But no matter how unpredictable the event, the ethnic hierarchy provides a reference for the development of primary relationships to help cope with its implications. This essentially reinforces the tendency to see the town and act towards it in terms of a flexible ethnic framework.

Because Papua New Guineans are from societies in which disputes are group matters, they act towards urban disputes collectively. Not having the personnel to re-form their own pre-existing groups in the towns, they seek wider bases of support. At the same time, other people are viewing them in terms of the wider identities provided by the terminological system, whose reality is reinforced not only by urban but national level developments. This is all further reinforced by the pervasive tendency in New Guinean social structure to turn relations of contiguity to ones of incorporation (cf. Barnes 1962). In the urban environment, where forces are at work to sort people from the same general area into similar socio-economic and residential niches, an ethnic construction of urban realities occurs which not only has the implications we have been stressing for primary relationships, but important general effects on the political and economic structures of the towns as well, which will be explored in the next chapter.

'Wantok', an urban social category

Although one may analytically distinguish between kinship, ethnicity and friendship (as we have above), we should stress that at the level of personal network formation these bases of social relationship are all used simultaneously as part of what Papua New Guineans call *wantok* ties. Living in town means becoming involved in new sorts of social relationships. As time goes on, urbanites meet and interact with more and more people who are not kinsmen and become greatly involved in the *wantok* system, a category of relationships that effectively combines kinship, ethnicity and more individualistic friendship ties in a new, pervasive urban social idiom.

Indeed, if one were to ask any urban Papua New Guineans seen in frequent contact with one another on social or recreational occasions to describe their relationship, they would most likely say they were *wantok*. This word, which may be used to denote partners in any primary relationship (except perhaps marriage), has been defined as 'one who speaks the same language, one who is of the same nationality, a compatriot, one who is from the same country, a neighbor' (Mihalic 1971: 202). In the case of kin, the term *wantok* is likely to be used to point out the primary nature of the tie to others. The kinsmen themselves would discuss their association in terms of their own group's cultural definitions (M. Strathern 1975: 298–9). In the case of what we would term simple (non-kin) friendship, the *wantok* would use the term between themselves as well as to outsiders. This ubiquitous urban category seems at first to be a very casual one, rather amorphously used as a greeting, an indication of friendship, kinship, ethnic commonality, etc. Exploring its use proves, however, that *wantok* relations form and are defined in rather consistent ways and, as we mentioned earlier, allows us to appreciate the way in which Papua New Guineans approach and differentiate between types of urban social relationships.

Perhaps the best way to introduce the reader to the meaning of the category is through informants' definitions. Asking individuals what *wantok* did that made them *wantok* elicited consistently the response that 'they stick together, converse frequently and eat together'. Courting, walking, working and washing together, sharing food, clothing and cigarettes (Seifert 1975: 75), are also things *wantok* do.

In general, then, the term may simply refer to frequent friendly interaction, but another point very often mentioned is that *wantok* come from the 'same place', a reference to their having a common village, province or (occasionally) region of origin. The farther one is from home, the wider the spatial referent.

Although it is generally recognized that the term may be extended to other than those of similar culture or area of origin, a distinction is made between 'true' *wantok* and what we might term 'honorary' *wantok*. An individual might say an acquaintance from an area not connected with his own (e.g. a European) is a *wantok*, 'but not a real *wantok*', or he might use the term in greeting a friendly stranger. Distinctions were also made between close and more distant *wantok*. These become apparent in the felt strength of the obligation to abide by normative elements of the *wantok* relationship. Sharing, mutual aid and defence are more often forthcoming from those one defines as close *wantok* in a particular situation than from those at the periphery of the category's range.

In addition to ease of interaction and common origin, another important element in this relationship, manifested by the consistent emphasis on mutuality and sharing, is the expectation that *wantok* will engage in ongoing transactions governed by 'generalised reciprocity' (Sahlins 1965). This is the key to understanding the apparently idiosyncratic usage of the term. It is worth noting that the present anthropological stress on the analytical importance of transactions in the understanding of social life (Barth 1966, Kapferer 1976) owes a great deal to Melanesianists. 'Melanesia is perhaps the region of the world in which the transactional character of social relationships is most prominent and this has been recognized since the accounts given by Seligman and Barton' (Brown 1970: 99). This is no less true of the towns than the rural areas. When exploring the history of particular urban friendships one is often met with statements such as 'I became his friend after he saw me on a bus and gave me five dollars', or 'He needed to have me to go to for money if an emergency came up'. This does not imply mercenary interests on the part of Papua New Guineans but a recognition that to be friends people must do things for one another in town. An initiating gift (e.g. the five dollars) and its acceptance are taken as an indication that a primary relationship is to proceed. Any breakdown of this reciprocity is likely to signal a rupturing of the relationship.

Anyone with whom such reciprocity is developed is a *wantok*, but some people are probable *wantok* by ascription (through facts of birth), while others may become so idiosyncratically in the course of urban life. There is a set of people in every urban social situation who are automatically recruitable *wantok* because they come from the flexibly defined 'same place'.[2] These people are 'natural' choices for friendships or primary relationships. Often they may be kin of kin, or just neighbours in town from the same province, who will seek each other out almost automatically (if brought within range by the urban system) to establish a base of potential support in time of need. If, on the other hand, fortuitous circumstances or interests arising out of an aspect of urban commonality leads to transactional sequences with other people, these too are *wantok* relationships. In either case, whether the *wantok* be kin, compatriots or met on the factory floor, transactions form the base on which the relationship is established. If for one reason or another the transactions cease, the relationship lapses – blood ties or common origin notwithstanding. We may wish to distinguish between the various bases of the '*wantok* system' (kinship, ethnicity and friendship), but should keep in mind the fact that 'primordial attachments' (Geertz 1963) do not make for automatic urban relationships. As Seifert noted for Chimbus in Goroka and Lae, exchanges mark the 'beginning of continuance of countless networks of relationships between individuals', and are 'a crucial factor in the process of adjustment to town life' (1975: 75). Although these exchanges are most likely to be arranged between kin or fellow ethnics, this by no means precludes other friendships being formed via the same mechanism.[3] All primary relationships depend on urban transactional sequences

[2] The *wantok* system seems to operate in ways similar to what are called 'home-boy' relationships in the literature on urban Africa. Harries-Jones states that 'The flexible use of the term *bakumwesu* on the Copperbelt means that residents could stress their "home-boy" ties in situations which called for the rendering of mutual services and indeed recognition of "home-boy" ties still implied reciprocal rights and duties' (1969: 340).

[3] People do occasionally cut themselves off from others by refusing to participate in this flow of prestations and become known as *wanpis* (loners). Town life permits individuals this option but very few take it (M. Strathern 1975: 147–8).

for their continuity. Their history and duration are then fundamentally affected by the factors that sort people out into different urban centres, housing areas and jobs, keep them circulating between village and town, etc.

A number of other points about the *wantok* system have been brought out. Rew (1974) and M. Strathern (1975) have mentioned cognitive aspects of this phenomenon. Noting that the town thrusts heterogeneity on to its workers, Rew states that the *wantok* system enables residents to deal with town events in a familiar way. Because of frequent returns to rural areas, and changes of job or address, many of these relationships are quite fragile. Nevertheless, 'their formation and death leave traces of underlying cultural understandings and conventions ... which serve to give meaning and at least minimal coherence to the Port Moresby social process' (1974: 28, 155), by providing knowledge and expectations concerning urban interactions.

The way in which Papua New Guineans categorize 'automatic' *wantok* also tells us something about the way in which they view the town. A Hagen, for example, may see himself as part of a *wantok* group composed of other Hagens, and views other people as belonging to similarly composed moral communities. This conception of the urban population as a replication of like units is also seen as a way of making sense of the urban environment, although it may be a more segmentary (or less integrated) view of it than westerners might hold (M. Strathern 1975: 289). Such a segmentary orientation is enabling as well as limiting. By staying within the bounds of the *wantok* system, one becomes encapsulated to a certain extent. But having this base of protection and security allows the urbanite to sample a variety of urban situations which might otherwise be too intimidating to approach and difficult to cope with (Rew 1974: 223).

To summarize, the migration process and urban environment make it difficult or impossible to use rural principles to re-create rural groups in towns. At the same time, however, the circulation of people between rural and urban areas, the urban housing and employment structures and the coincidence of skills, education and area of origin due to the variable impact of colonialism, 'fail to interdigitate the population and encourage importation of rural ties' (Rew 1974: 224). In the case of kinship these ties may themselves have pre-dated urban residence although, as we have seen, urban kinship is a phenomenon in its own right.

Although the urban system itself encourages or enables relationships to form which have rural referents, as one moves beyond the range of kinship to the use of the idioms of ethnicity and the *wantok* system, many new social ties are created. It is important to emphasize that these are not pre-existing relationships. Despite the continuity with rural styles evident in transactional patterns or reference to the 'home' area, rural groupings give way to new, more eclectic and inclusive urban social networks which become the basis of the formation of social aggregations fundamentally different from those which exist in traditional Melanesian society.

As we shall see in the next chapter, these networks and the principles that underlie their formation importantly condition social action in the wider urban field as well as the more personal social realm we have emphasized in this chapter.

5. Social idioms in the wider urban field

In the last chapter we examined social idioms and the residential situation of Papua New Guinean urbanites as contexts in which they developed bases of personal security in towns. These bases were said to be essential aspects of urbanization permitting entry into what we have called the wider urban social field. Perhaps the most compelling aspect of that social field is the world of work, one that draws Papua New Guineans into new roles and relationships presenting great potential for social change. In the opening sections of this chapter we will look at what sorts of employment urbanites are involved in, some of their work situations, and the effects of socio-economic position on social consciousness and group formation.

The general urban employment situation

As we have mentioned in a previous chapter, until the late 1950s urban Papua New Guineans were employed almost exclusively as unskilled labour (the major exceptions being the inhabitants of villages within the boundaries of towns like Port Moresby and Rabaul, who were commonly engaged in the sale of goods and services to the town, or subsistence activities or both). This situation changed substantially in the early 1960s when the Australian administration began employing many more Papua New Guineans in higher-level positions with a view towards preparing the country for independence. But although public employment of indigenes increased by over 40 per cent between 1962 and 1964 (Garnaut forthcoming), their movement into skilled and professional positions was a good bit slower in gathering momentum – understandably so, perhaps, as the first high schools were not developed until 1957 and the university in 1966 (Wolfers 1976: 21). For example, by 1966 in Port Moresby, 58 per cent of the work-force was involved in unskilled labour (i.e. domestic work, grass cutting, stevedoring, etc.), 30 per cent were semi-skilled (drivers, shop assistants, factory workers), 11 per cent skilled (tradesmen, clerks, technicians) and 1.5 per cent professional and managerial. By 1971 the proportion in professional and managerial positions had more than doubled to 3.5 per cent, the proportion in skilled occupations had nearly quadrupled to 41.5 per cent, 18 per cent were semi-skilled and 37 per cent were unskilled. The approximate proportions for Papua New Guinea's major urban areas taken together (according to the June 1971 census) are 6.5 per cent professional and managerial, 35 per cent skilled, 20 per cent semi-skilled and 40 per cent unskilled. It has been suggested that the available data play down the real state of occupational advancement since indigenous public servants were commonly spending 'long periods of time acting in positions well above their substantive position so as to gain experience to withstand appeals from longer-serving permanent expatriate officers' (Wolfers 1976: 22).

While government employment opportunities for local people grew rapidly from the early 1960s, the private sector experienced accelerated employment growth under the five-year development programme of 1968 (with increased private investment in mining, construction, manufacturing, commerce, tourism, etc.). The public sector accounted for about half the growth in employment in the major urban areas, although the private sector was especially important in Lae (with its growing manufacturing industries), Mount Hagen (which services the expanding Western Highlands Province) and the mining towns of Bougainville (Garnaut forthcoming). According to the 1971 census, government employees made up about 30 per cent of the urban work-force, while the private sector accounted for the rest. In the latter there has been a significant shift from formal employment agreements to casual employment (ibid.). A survey of 114 businesses has shown that the private sector has followed the government in its localization policies, 44 per cent of the responding enterprises having Papua New Guineans in senior executive positions (compared with 26 per cent in 1975) while 49 per cent said they would be appointing more into executive posts in 1977 (Papua New Guinea Newsletter, 21 January 1977). Localization and the movement of Papua New Guineans into higher and better-paid positions, together with the increase in the urban minimum wage and public servants' salaries, made it more possible for migrants to have their wives and families together with them in town, thus pushing the urban sex and age distribution towards the national averages.

Although wage employment continues to be by far the most important source of income for urban Papua New Guineans, the *proportion* of employed people in the towns has decreased partly because of the above-mentioned demographic shift. Furthermore, urban wage employment in itself ceased to expand in the early 1970s, partly because very low commodity prices cut back rural incomes and thus reduced the hinterland demand for goods and services from the towns, but also because of uncertainty within the business community prior to the 1972 elections concerning policies of the national coalition government. The employment of domestic servants dropped as expatriates continued to leave the country in the wake of increasing localization. Non-government related building and construction declined, as did manufacturing aimed at expatriate consumption and investment; but employment in public sector building and construction increased in preparation for self-government and independence, as did the manufacture of consumer goods for the indigenous market, such as food, beer and clothing. Government employment of day-labourers, which increased in 1972, declined over the following two years in response to budget restraints and rising urban wage levels. Nevertheless, the government's overall employment level has continued to increase since 1971 and it remains by far the largest single employer in the country (Garnaut forthcoming).

Work roles and the work situation

Relatively little research has been done on the performance of work roles in urban Papua New Guinea or on any other aspects of the work situation. Some information does exist on employer–employee relationships, the problems attendant on localization, inter-ethnic work relationships and the role of the *wantok* system in a number of different work settings.

The evidence of Salisbury (1967), M. Strathern (1975) and our own informants seems to indicate that there sometimes is a real difference between the way an expatriate employer and an indigenous employee perceive the worker's role, especially in the case of domestic servants. Both Sianes and Hagens in urban employment are said to view themselves as more than just employees. Hagens see themselves as working for *someone* and 'phrase the desire for higher wages in terms of recognition from the employer' (M. Strathern 1975: 135). Siane domestic servants regard their European employers as 'big-men' according to Salisbury, and themselves as supporters. As such, the domestic sees himself as collaborating with his employer to run the household. He

comes in and does things around *his* house; ... brags ... about the wonderful parties *we* (he and his employer) threw ... But if it is *his* party he will want to act as co-giver, helping with preparations and tasting odds and ends. He will come round at odd hours and participate in all sorts of things that [his employer] may not want him to participate in (Salisbury 1967: 4).

Many Europeans are unprepared to accept this sort of familiarity on the part of a Highlands domestic. A number of our informants had no end of trouble with expatriate females, especially if the women stayed at home while they were working. Drinking the household's beer, borrowing some of the husband's clothing and bringing kin and friends around for a smoke led to wrangling which increased in tempo until the lady of the house persuaded her husband to fire the person, or did so herself. However, those few Europeans whose sense of propriety was not overly violated and could accept such behaviour, and had an interest in meeting the worker's family and friends (or at least tolerated them), would find they had a firm supporter. Those domestics we knew who worked for such expatriates often extended kin terms to them, looked after their children at night without asking for extra pay, guarded the house when the family was away, etc. Some ties were very close, and a few domestics have been sent airline tickets to visit their former employers in Australia. An identification with the employer, his household and standing, similar to that reported by Salisbury, seemed to develop if the employer did not discourage it.

Rew, in his study of a company in Port Moresby, found that the relationship between employers and employee, and between expatriates and indigenes, depended largely on the worker's specific position in the enterprise and was influenced by the trend towards localization.

The policy of the company was gradually to localize all positions except for those of a few senior officers. This was in keeping with the political climate and the fact that the enterprise was growing and indigenes could be paid much less than expatriates. Thus employees who worked with senior managerial staff were dealing with people who were seriously concerned with good inter-racial relationships and the future of the firm. European manual labourers had no such concerns as they were on short-term contracts, and economically and occupationally were in competition with their Papua New Guinean workmates (1974: 38–9, 76).

There were six indigenes for every European employed by the company, but those involved in the actual production process tended to have less contact with expatriates than those in the ancillary sections. Quality control and the regulation of production flow were automatic and impersonal, while day-to-day routine supervision was in the hands of indigenous shift supervisors and a trainee foreman. There was more personal control and supervision over office workers and men involved in transport, which Rew describes as continuous and kindly in the case of the desk workers (half of which were expatriate) and as intermittent and less kindly with respect to the truck drivers and 'truck boys' (ibid.: 33–4).

In the course of recruiting indigenous workers, the company found no shortage of unskilled and semi-skilled applicants and displayed no particular interest in their placement. Employees would often present their kinsmen for these positions and they would be hired on the spot (ibid.: 37–40). In this way a number of firms have had discrete sections of their body of employees entirely filled with migrants from a particular area of the country. For example, all the garbage collectors in the main rubbish hauling company in Port Moresby are Goilalas (Metcalfe 1968: 58), while in Lae this niche is filled by Chimbus (Zimmerman 1973: 91).

For more skilled positions, the management would be more selective, placing new recruits with co-ethnics for on-the-job training in self-managing task groups. The workers would be under a 'line-boss', the oldest worker, who would pass on his skills to the new men. With increasing localization of higher positions, the management became more interested than ever in raising the standard of their recruits, demanding certification and references. They found, however, that the line-boss system, useful as it was for on-the-job training, could seriously interfere with management's policies if the line-boss decided not to co-operate in the training of any particular recruit. (This happened when a New Guinean was allocated to a task group of Gulf District Papuans.) Management's hegemony was less likely to be challenged in those groups which were heterogeneous both ethnically and educationally (Rew 1974: 37–40).

It is interesting to note that, in contrast to the kind of expatriate-owned concern that Rew describes, there is less formal organization of the workers in businesses owned and run by Papua New Guineans. For example, indigenous contractors organize their men into task groups or work gangs but let them take on a variety of types of jobs, while expatriates seem to trust locals with only one kind of job (like steel work or pouring concrete) to which each gang would be restricted. In Papua New Guinean run factories, an individual worker's tasks are not so fixed as in European firms, and there is more room for assigning different sorts of jobs (Andrews 1975: 61).

Localization has also been of major concern to the police and the army who are garrisoned in urban areas. In 1966 there began a large-scale expansion of the police force and an effort to improve standards and raise the level of knowledge, initiative and expertise among indigenous staff. This overhaul resulted in the replacement of a number of senior expatriate men by local commissioned officers (mostly in their twenties), and the growth of a body of young, more literate constables. Tufman (1974) suggests that this programme has not been entirely successful: 'Many, perhaps even the majority of indigenous policemen, lack the knowledge, confidence and initiative which provide for competence.' He points to inadequate training (four years for officers and six months for constables) as an important reason for this.

According to Ranson (1972: 38–41), the fact that the older married police tend to be less well educated makes their effective employment in the town situation problematical, as they are called upon to cope with a racially, ethnically and educationally heterogeneous population. Where these men have long service records, and have advanced in rank, there is often some hostility between them and more recent recruits who are younger and better educated. In addition, although members of the force seem to like their work on the whole, they tend to worry about the inadequacy of their pay in light of high costs in the towns (especially Port Moresby) and poor on-post living conditions (especially for married men). Job satisfaction is also reduced by the fact that there is a 'lack of public respect for the job being done', particularly the enforcement of the (recently repealed) laws against card-playing.

Oram (1976: 226–9) sees internal maladministration, the rapidity of localization, a lack of individual experience, technical equipment and training, as well as isolation from the community at large, as factors lying behind the poor performance, image and morale of Port Moresby's police.

Tufman further argues that 'allegiance to clan is another factor militating against the efficiency of the Police. Occasionally off-duty policemen will go to the aid of a civilian "wantok" who is about to be arrested, thus severely undermining public confidence in the Force' (1974: 88).

The army has been localizing the positions of senior non-commissioned officers and junior officers since 1963. More recently the rate of indigenization has been increased by sending more cadets to Officer Training School in Australia and by the experimental commissioning of senior NCOs after a three-month training course.

O'Neill (1971) argues that superior administration and training make the army the true Papua New Guinean élite despite the fact that the administration insists that wages and accommodation remain in line with those of public servants and police. The army has no difficulty in getting top-flight Australian officers to come to Papua New Guinea as some prestige has come to be attached to this assignment. Furthermore, the small turnover and great demand for vacancies allows the Pacific Islands Regiment to set a high standard for recruits. The threat of dismissal is taken seriously by the troops, making for stricter discipline. Recruitment from the various parts of the country is made proportionate to census population. In order to ensure sufficient representation for certain areas of the Highlands, educational standards are occasionally lowered. According to Bell (1967), the detribalizing influences of such an integrated force result in cross-ethnic personal friendships and a diminution of inter-tribal prejudices. It is interesting to note, however, that an army *wantok*-based line system exists, similar to that described by Rew, which is also seen as an impediment to the goals of the institution as a whole (i.e. integration). It seems to be something of a holdover, though, since the line-boss tends to be more influential with older soldiers than with the younger, better-educated recruits.

Although *wantok* relationships may be decreasing in importance within the army, Bell suggests that the troops still maintain close links with their villages and commonly plan to retire there to be cared for in their old age. But even these attitudes may be changing. The two army men in Whiteman's sample of Chimbus living in Port Moresby reportedly avow that 'a soldier's social relationships should be with other soldiers rather than with his own tribesmen and that in times of need, the army rather than his kinsmen would take care of him' (1973: 78). Bell goes so far as to suggest that the army may be becoming a tribe in itself (1967: 58).

Ballard (1976) takes up some of these same issues in his discussion of attitudes to *wantok* in the administration. He argues that *wantok* ties can be profitably exploited in a number of ways. For example, the *wantok* network of upper-echelon public servants has made for more efficient co-operation between government departments. Mono-ethnic *wantok* ties in the lower echelons make working within the bureaucracy inherited from the Australian administration a pleasanter and less alienating experience. Most importantly, co-ethnic ties between those inside the administration and their kin on the outside makes the government's services more accessible to Papua New Guineans who might not otherwise have the sophistication and skills necessary for dealing effectively with the bureaucracy and its red tape. Ballard also mentions some possible abuses of the *wantok* system, such as preferential treatment of co-ethnics, and the problem of government élites 'scratching each others' backs' on the national and local level. In addition, the effective lobbying of the Public Servants' Association (which Ballard considers to be a sort of *wantok* group) has kept up and even increased the rolls of government employees in the face of stringent cut-backs in departmental budgets.

We may argue then, that the employment of the *wantok* idiom by Papua New Guinean townsmen is not only adaptive in terms of mediating the urban environment by providing community and personal security, but can also be useful in the work situation. The existence of *wantok* ties with work-mates can function as a basis for co-operation on the job, as in the case of the line-boss system used in the Port Moresby company and the army (although the goals of these *wantok* groups may sometimes conflict with those of the institution within which they work). The existence of such ties between workers and people outside the institution can, on the one hand, provide for better extension services (as, for example, when the government bureaucracy is thus made more open to public access), while on the other hand, it may lead to preferences which interfere with the very working of the institution in question (as when the police avoid arresting their *wantok* and thus damage their reputation with the wider urban population).

When the *wantok* idiom is extended to embrace work-mates of a similar educational background or work experience, as is the case with some government department heads and senior officers, this enables the creation of informal networks which greatly expedite the workings of a bureaucracy. When these ties are extended more or less throughout an institution, as may be occurring in the army, they can make for great *esprit de corps* (not to mention extraordinarily exciting Police versus Army rugby games). It may even be possible that the general extension of *wantok* links to co-workers could in future lay the foundation for some style of effective collective action towards job-related goals.

Thus urban Papua New Guineans continue to apply and adapt some of the same idioms which we discussed in the previous chapter to the work situation with varying results and degrees of success, for themselves, for the institutions they work in, and, by implication, for the towns as a whole.

The issue of class formation

Now that we have an idea of the overall role and distribution of Papua New Guineans in the urban economy, and have discussed some of the ways in which work situations are approached by them, an interesting general sociological question to consider is whether or not new ideologies develop out of the work situation and significantly alter the consciousness, principles and idioms of group formation used by urban Papua New Guineans. Such questions are fundamental to an understanding of urbanization and have been addressed by scholars in other areas of the Third World for some time. Epstein (1958), for example, has shown how in the African mine compound of Luanshya, Zambia, 'tribalism' (a basis of personal and domestic relations) was replaced by the formation of class-oriented groups in the industrial sphere.

The main thrust of our last chapter was, of course, to show how kinship and ethnicity were used to carve out spheres of security and, specifically, to establish personal and domestic social relations. We have also seen, in this last section, how these principles continue to be important in the work situation as well. But in looking towards the wider urban field as a whole, the question arises of whether the increasing participation of Papua New Guineans in the urban economy is creating social categories that become the foci of competing interest groups which develop an internal solidarity based on their common economic position. Or do the previously discussed principles of association prevent, distort or cross-cut this?

In order to address such issues we should begin by discussing certain general ideas on the formation of classes and class consciousness and the meaning of 'proletarian'. A point which will emerge from this is that both objective and subjective factors enter into discussions of class. Having already delineated a general picture of the objective background, we may turn in the following sections to a consideration of the meaning this situation has for Papua New Guineans and how they approach a western-based system of social differentiation: what they make of it and what it makes of them. Some relevant questions to be taken up include: How do people view and evaluate the urban socio-economic hierarchy? Are they committed to their jobs and do they gain satisfaction from them? If certain positions in the socio-economic hierarchy are seen as more desirable than others, do people allocate prestige to themselves and others on the basis of these positions? Do the upwardly mobile continue to abide by norms of sharing and status equivalence with *wantok*, or do they attempt to cut themselves off from such obligations? How do these factors affect mobility and the development of solidarity along class lines?

Class 'in itself', 'for itself' and proletarianization

These concepts, which have proved so influential in the history of modern sociology (and politics), were developed in the writings of Karl Marx. 'A social class in Marx's terms is any aggregate of persons who perform the same function in the organisation of production' (Bendix and Lipset 1967: 7). In this sense, class is an objective phenomenon. In Papua New Guinean towns it is not difficult to distinguish between people on the basis of their respective positions in the economy and there is no doubt that in an objective sense class exists. Thus in Madang, for example, 'each stratum has a specific "class situation" sharing similar relations to the market, similar life chances' (Stevenson 1968: 133).

In the colonial period most Papua New Guineans were unskilled workers, and expatriates controlled virtually the entire urban economy. Although expatriate economic dominance is still apparent today, an indigenous government now has ultimate control over the nation's resources and, as we have pointed out in the previous sections, local-ization policy has ensured that Papua New Guineans are moving further up the socio-economic hierarchy. At this point in time it is no longer possible to say that natives form a working class and expatriates a ruling class. The objective situation is far more complicated than that. Position in the economic system is now a valid basis of distinction amongst the indigenous population. As we have seen, life chances in town are indeed different for residents of different housing areas who tend to be separated into them primarily on the basis of their place in the economic system.

If we were to begin demarcating classes in urban Papua New Guinea on the basis of job, income and associated life-style, we might be able to derive a fairly accurate set of socio-economic distinctions with which to sort out the urban population. This might be a useful exercise for certain purposes (e.g. town planning or advertising) but we could not auto-matically assume that categories we construct would be meaningful to Papua New Guineans. Marx felt that class position 'provided the crucial life experience which would determine, either now or eventually, the beliefs and the actions of the individual' (Bendix and Lipset 1967: 8). As such, class is also a subjective phenomenon which enters into the consciousness of people. When individuals come to realize their objective class position and act collectively upon it to better their life chances, mere position in the economy is transformed into a principle of social identity and solidarity, 'class for itself'. It is only when this occurs that true classes form. Prior to such realization, members in the same objective economic position (class *in* itself) may be on hostile terms with each other as competitors for the same jobs.

The crucial question for Papua New Guinea is whether this class consciousness has occurred, or is occurring, or whether the fragmentation and competition of the objective class situation is reinforced by idioms such as those of the *wantok* system. When Marx wrote about the development of classes in Europe he stressed a number of factors which developed over a long period of time to create a proletariat or working class. The industrial economy which brings people from a wide hinterland and concentrates them in an urban area takes them away from their land and other sources of livelihood. The worker then becomes dependent for survival solely on the ability to sell his labour in the market-place. These developments do not of course occur overnight and, as we know, Papua New Guineans are not permanently separated from their land since they do circulate between town and country fairly regularly. But while they are in town, the only way to earn steady cash is to work and the worker's only value to his employer is his labour. In certain situations, then, the Papua New Guinean worker is in a position similar to a western industrial worker. This should have some effect on the consciousness and behaviour of urbanites. But proletarianization and class consciousness in Papua New Guinea, although sometimes apparent, are not yet well developed because of a constellation of factors involved with the urbanization process, which we will take up below.

Occupational prestige, attitudes towards employment, job circulation

Available literature seems to indicate that Papua New Guinean school-leavers accord the greatest prestige to the jobs which provide the highest income (Conroy 1973: 15). The relatively few studies of this subject, done with workers and others, point to some more interesting trends, however. Perhaps the most suggestive information involves reports by researchers investigating occupational prestige, which deal with the difficulty of getting Papua New Guineans to provide information on rankings in the first place. Epstein (1967), for example, found a high degree of variation in the rankings of occupations by Tolai peri-urban villagers on the Gazelle Peninsula, who were engaged in wage-work and cash-cropping. Agricultural occupations ranked highest but there were a large number of 'don't know' responses. He suggested that the overall pattern is indicative of a general lack of occupational differentiation.

Rew, in his study of some workers in Port Moresby, found that professions (teaching and medicine) were the most highly rated occupations and unskilled work the least. Skilled manual work was in some cases accorded greater prestige than white-collar jobs. Driving was especially highly rated by Highlanders. 'Yet orthogonal to this general tendency was an undercurrent of rejection of wage employment on the whole, certain respondents preferring business occupations. These were seen as unequivocally centered in the rural areas' (1974: 180). Rew showed his informants a series of photographs depicting local people at work and asked them to rank them in terms of prestige. Some people refused to co-operate saying that the task was boring. In other situations groups gathered and general banter intervened. Other people said they liked certain photos or in other ways appeared to misunderstand the task (ibid.: 175).

When M. Strathern decided to study occupational prestige among Port Moresby's Hageners she used Rew's photographs as an instrument in an attempt to provide a controlled comparison. But her informants refused to rank the pictures and stressed they would not speak for community opinion. They said some jobs were good for some people and others good for other people. Strathern sees this refusal as evidence of a lack of perception of an all-inclusive urban socio-economic hierarchy, which fits in with the aforementioned segmentary view Hageners have of urban society. She also stresses that in industrial societies a series of predetermined values operate in such exercises which urban Hageners do not have (1975: 308). Although they would not rank the pictures they do wish to get licences and become drivers, much preferring this to outside labour such as grass cutting. Skilled individuals are likely to have a high opinion of their particular jobs (ibid.: 113–14).

The stress on driving, which has been noted for Highlanders by Rew (1974), Salisbury and Salisbury (1972), M. Strathern (1975) and Levine (1976), is due to the fact (as the people themselves point out) that driving is the skill most accessible to them in town which is also useful in the rural area. The cumulative impression of the results of attempts to elicit ideas about job prestige seems to support Rew's conclusions, although there is a good deal of hesitation and uncertainty involved which shows that people are not used to grading their occupations carefully vis-à-vis others.

M. Strathern (1975: 329) says that Hageners do not even compare wages across jobs. Bad conditions and low pay are blamed on their specific employer and are not seen as reflections of their class. Rather than view their situation in terms of impersonal industrially oriented relationships, Hageners, as mentioned in the previous section, tend to create a dyadic tie with an employer, seeing it as involving reciprocal obligations. (Salisbury (1967) makes much the same point.)

Stevenson notes that the factory hands he studied in Madang developed a strong sense of deprivation and antagonism towards employers (1968: 133). These reactions are quite understandable in light of the poor conditions many labourers work under, their powerlessness and the degradation experienced at the hands of cavalier expatriate employers, who often seem to have a 'take it or leave it' attitude as far as working conditions and pay are concerned. But if the situation as described for Hageners is a general one, and if specific bosses rather than 'the system' are seen as the culprits, then the workers (however alienated) are unlikely to join together and form a united front. The most common form of protest, mentioned by Stevenson and M. Strathern, is to quit. Rather than acknowledge their powerlessness, Hageners bypass the hierarchy and the wider implications of their socio-economic position by emphasizing their independence. Workers in Madang are in a constant state of flux and leave their jobs when they have had enough, stressing that their ties with the village and *wantok* permit them to do this (M. Strathern 1975, Stevenson 1968: 118). Having an 'out', be it the village or their urban *wantok*, allows the townsmen (who may appear to an outsider to be desperately impoverished, overworked and underpaid) to say that their employer had better take them on their own terms or they will just up and leave. Urban Papua New Guineans often do so, very much on the spur of the moment (Levine 1976).

Bedford and Mamak (1976), however, have noted that certain urbanites in Bougainville may be more committed to wage-work than others. People whose villages are near Panguna alternate between work in town and cash-cropping. They are the group most dissatisfied with their (by-and-large) unskilled jobs, but because they view them as temporary, they do not join unions. Those from the isolated interior of Bougainville, on the other hand, become more involved in urban associations as their limited opportunities for cash-cropping and for maintaining ties with their villages mean that they must remain in town to earn money. But even here 'ultimate achievement of economic success in a rural rather than urban context is still the primary consideration'. Improved road networks are likely to facilitate rural–urban circularity on Bougainville and encourage strategies aimed at dual (urban and rural) participation (ibid.: 186–7).

These comments apply primarily to the unskilled workers studied by most authors. The skilled seem to have more definite ideas about the relative prestige of their jobs and view themselves as being involved in wage-work for the rest of their working lives (Levine 1976, Rew 1974, M. Strathern 1975).

The general tendency towards an ideological distance from the world of work and the hierarchy it involves workers in has great consequences for both class formation and the urban economy in general. From the point of view of the employment market there is a great deal of job circulation apparent in the towns. Various accounts of the work histories of particular men (e.g. in Levine 1976) show an extraordinary number of moves both within the town (from employer to employer) and between town and village for varying periods. Rew (1974: 184) and M. Strathern (1975: 118–36) present detailed data on the circulation of large numbers of their informants which also demonstrate a great deal of movement. As an example, we may take the case of a Hagener, James, living in Port Moresby whose account of his own work history (M. Strathern 1975: 118–22) we will summarize. (Indications of time are only rough approximations.)

He got his first job after being in town for three weeks. It was a temporary one, preparing a garden, and only lasted for a couple of months, but a letter of reference led to three similar short-term appointments. After this he worked alongside a clan brother on the university work gang. When his *wantok* was dismissed eight months later, James decided to quit and spent the next month as a *pasendia*. He then found a job as a houseboy (paying $12 a fortnight) but was dismissed after one month for incompetence. With his next position (domestic work, as was all his subsequent employment) he was given sleeping quarters and paid $14 per fortnight. But when this employer refused to give him the raise he asked for after over two years' service, James decided to leave, collecting the $150 he had saved and that his employer's wife had banked for him. At his next job he got $20 a fortnight but slept in the quarters of Ivan, a clansman, and had to take a bus to where he worked. The couple he kept house for left for work at seven o'clock every morning and did not give him a spare key, so he had several altercations with the wife when he got to work late and was finally dismissed after ten months' employment. When one of the three bachelors that Ivan (his host) worked for got married, James went to work for him, but was paid only $12 per fortnight and left after three months. Now he was unemployed for a month, staying with Ivan again. His next job lasted three months – the lady of the house was pleasant enough, but the servants' quarters were in serious disrepair. He was *pasendia* for a week, but no longer stayed with Ivan. He next worked for a woman who looked after children; he was given a great deal of washing and ironing to do and left after a month. He was *pasendia* for two weeks, then went to work for three women who paid him $8 per week. When one of them left the house two months later, the others reduced his pay to $6 a week and he quit. Again *pasendia*, his host told him that he might find work next door but this only lasted a month as he got into a fight with his employer while drunk. He had not found work since.

Not all of this occupational instability is a result of the workers' ideology or dissatisfaction. For example, domestic servants frequently find themselves involuntarily out of work when their expatriate employers leave town because they get transferred, localized or go on leave overseas. In general, it is evident from these studies that the mobility involved in these shifts is horizontal. The unskilled remain in unskilled positions except for periods of unemployment.

The data available on occupational prestige, attitudes towards work, and job circulation seem to indicate a reluctance to acknowledge an occupational prestige hierarchy, a dissatisfaction with unskilled work which is expressed in frequent resignations, and an undercurrent of rejection of urban wage-labour supported by statements of intention to go home, actual returns to village areas, and the high value placed on obtaining skills and experience relevant to rural business activity.

Socio-economic position and personal status

Although two authors cited in the last section elicited information which seems to indicate that income, the professions and skilled manual trades are valued by urban workers, we have seen that Papua New Guineans are reluctant to rank jobs. But even if the information on Hageners' lack of a hierarchical model of industrial positions is generally true, Papua New Guineans might nonetheless accord status to people with high incomes regardless of what they think about general occupational categories. In other words, their negative response to sociological questionnaires or projective tests on an abstract series of positions does not in itself preclude a coincidence of socio-economic status and personal prestige. If the unskilled worker is consistently denied prestige by others, worker solidarity might be expected to increase. If, on the other hand, status equivalence is stressed across socio-economic lines, the potential for such solidarity may be diminished.

It is quite obvious that many expatriate employers feel inherently superior to their unskilled workers. Stevenson relates how the shame workers feel vis-à-vis expatriates prevents them from asking for better working conditions. Employers seeing a great many men asking for work can easily dispense with unskilled employees if they complain, and need not propitiate them in any way. The ordinary worker resents not only the fact that he does all the hard work for little pay while making the employer's business grow, but also that he is often treated without regard to his humanity. Stevenson quotes factory workers in Madang who stress their resentment at being valued on a par with disposable objects, pigs or dogs, by bosses who stand around all day doing nothing strenuous. They want better pay *and* recognition of equality. Skilled workers seemed more concerned with the fact that, although they are equal to expatriates in terms of job skills, education, and performance, whites and blacks do not get equal pay for equal work (1968: 115, 123–4, 128, 131). Such attitudes might, especially in colonial times, have been an important spur to worker solidarity. But now that European domination is diminishing, stressing anti-expatriate attitudes tends to play down the existence of an indigenous socio-economic status hierarchy. It would be very interesting to know how Papua New Guineans treat their workers, but unfortunately there have been too few indigenes in the role of employer to have had a cumulative effect, or to allow one to make generalizations.

In any case, now that socio-economic status differentiation among Papua New Guineans exists, it is also important to know what effect this has on individual prestige outside working hours. For example, our own informants frequently disparaged poorly dressed people collecting bottles along the road as 'rubbishmen' or worthless individuals. As we have seen in the section on urban settlements, the status of a 'passenger' is rather marginal. University students frequently talk of themselves as the nation's élite, and educated people generally expect to become important both in the urban society in general and among their own kin. However, most negative evaluations of others that are expressed in terms of socio-economic position are aimed at people from other groups, who are not *wantok*. When there is no tie of kinship or common ethnicity in terms of which to evaluate a person, their socio-economic status may be stressed to a far greater extent than if they are compatriots. In the latter case, position in the emerging socio-economic hierarchy may be only one of a number of criteria relevant to overall personal prestige.

What we are suggesting is that socio-economic categories may be considerably more relevant in situations involving inter-ethnic interaction than among *wantok*. This generalization is supported by a number of statements in the local literature. Whiteman notes that 'expatriates and well-educated Papua New Guineans accord high status to educated western-oriented Chimbu and low status to uneducated, low-level income Chimbu', classifying them in terms of the same status concepts used in western society. Chimbu themselves, however, 'excepting perhaps the most highly educated, do not give status in terms of education or occupation but in terms of what people are doing for their social group'. Generosity, not income, is what earns one prestige (1973: 44). M. Strathern states that, although the attitudes of skilled Hagen migrants are 'more clearly formulated in relation to the outside world', when they interact with *wantok* they are treated 'almost without reference to their position in the urban economy'. Work position is considered unique to the employment situation 'and is not seen to extend outside it' (1975: 306–9).

Another relevant aspect of status concerns the pattern of transactions which go on among *wantok*. In traditional Melanesian society, an imbalance in transaction is associated with an imbalance in prestige, the giver's name going 'on top' of that of the receiver. We may be able to learn something about relative status in the towns by examining the transactions between urbanites. We may also ask whether or not the transactions themselves result in such a redistribution of resources that income differentials are substantially levelled. Do we have a situation where skilled or high-income workers are able to arrange jobs for unskilled *wantok*, or give them significant financial aid, thus deriving a traditional type of prestige from their high socio-economic status? Or do they choose to cut themselves off from their compatriots and become a westernized élite divorced from a tribalized proletariat?

With reference to the redistribution of incomes, Lucas (1972: 274) argues that the employed are rarely well off because unemployed people are a 'continual drain on their resources'. This would suggest that some levelling of income differentials occurs, but is it across socio-economic lines? Our own skilled informants in Port Moresby remained attached to their *wantok* and contributed money primarily on occasions when group resources were mobilized. One study, which presents budget information on thirteen low-covenant families earning better than average salaries in Port Moresby, shows that 14 per cent of their total expenditure was on gifts, not including food and stimulants which are often shared between relatives (Oeser 1969: 74, 76). However, it seems (from our informants and the scant mention of skilled workers in other studies) that such individuals spend somewhat less time in the company of unskilled *wantok* and a smaller proportion of their income on them than do the less well placed. While they do not actually sever relations and often help close kin with monetary gifts, much of the gift giving or money transmitted to kinsmen goes to the village area and visitors rather than to townsmen. Although a certain amount of income levelling does occur, it is not enough to make socio-economic equals of all urban *wantok*.

Such economic differences, pregnant as they may be with potential for change, are played down in encounters between skilled and unskilled compatriots. We found that, being younger, our skilled informants often took a back seat during ceremonial occasions, deferring to more knowledgeable elders. Nevertheless, these skilled and educated migrants may have a certain prestige within their ethnic group which seems to stem from the fact that they have more contacts with outsiders and know their way around the town and its alien institutions better than their *wantok*. An informant reported that when he first came to Port Moresby as a young army recruit, people whom he had never met before, but who came from his home district (the Western Highlands), went out of their way to present him with gifts and make him a part of their social network. Oeser found that although gift giving and receiving were not associated with income, there was definitely a pattern of giving gifts to people who had a large number of urban associations (relationships with individuals outside their own language group) and who scored high on a composite urban capability scale (designed to measure 'the ability to cope with *urban* problems, people and experiences') (1969: 73). People who are able to get others jobs may be well thought of but they do not become patrons as they rarely ultimately control the position to which they recruit *wantok* (Levine 1976, M. Strathern 1975). The prestige that does accrue to the skilled or educated migrant comes not from his high income or position *per se*, but from his ability to help his *wantok* 'work the system'.

It seems from the above that one must distinguish between socio-economic status in the sense of an encompassing hierarchy of positions in the economy, and 'status group', a concept developed by Weber. Status to Weber refers to social honour or the lack of it, and is conditioned and expressed through style of life (1966: 31–2). In urban Papua New Guinea, *wantok* cliques operate status concepts which in many situations refer to honour in terms of traditional skills. A village big-man living in town, entrusted with the responsibility of arranging for bodies to be sent home, adjudicating disputes between kin, etc., may be a 'passenger' in a poor-quality settlement residence. To his *wantok* he remains an important person, although to others he may appear to be an old rubbishman (Levine 1976). Honour may be found in *wantok* groups in terms of non-urban skills while inter-ethnic encounters take more account of socio-economic position. While the skilled and educated can find respect in interaction with both *wantok* and outsiders, the unskilled labourer can avoid the distress of low socio-economic status by remaining with his *wantok*. This *wantok* solidarity has significance for the development of class consciousness as we will see in the next section.

Class consciousness

The existence of egalitarian urban *wantok* networks which assume important roles as status and reference groups, together with the tendency to use socio-economic differences as status markers in inter-ethnic encounters, creates pressures for and against the development of class solidarity.

Rural idioms and modes of behaviour, and an ideological commitment to going home, are urban phenomena which also fundamentally detract from the development of class solidarity, particularly for unskilled workers. We have cited Bedford and Mamak (1976) on the lack of commitment to active betterment of working conditions on the part of Bougainvilleans who feel they can, when they like, opt out of the urban socio-economic system. Speaking of young single barracks dwellers, Rew concludes that 'the centripetal force of rural involvements was greater than the centrifugal force of urban involvement', even though this pattern was subject to change as urban residence lengthened (1974: 135). Workers who plan to go home are more concerned with maintaining relationships with *wantok* and visitors whose interests lie in the same rural area. If membership in *wantok* groups does not reinforce the implications of the urban socio-economic hierarchy, and the group provides a refuge from it for the worker, the chances for a 'class struggle' are lessened.

On the job, in actual work situations, ethnicity may serve to fragment the work-force when it becomes an idiom of solidarity or dispute. The more heterogeneous section of a Port Moresby company was the one that showed the least internal social solidarity, while the all-Kerema work section was much more closely knit and able to thwart the firm's introduction of New Guineans into their work line (Rew 1974: 29). Stevenson also has noted that strife between *wantok* groups divides the work-force against itself and prevents the emergence of worker solidarity. Where *wantok* are able to procure jobs for one another, often in institutions with a high labour turnover (M. Strathern 1975: 152), such groups may be in active conflict over access to positions. Competition in these instances may be on a very specific basis (e.g. between kin or village groups from a discrete area of origin, as has been reported from Madang) (Stevenson 1968: 122).

The tendency towards a regional pattern of socio-economic differentiation developing out of the colonial experience (mentioned in Chapter Two) sometimes leads individuals to perceive the emerging hierarchy in ethnic terms. This may (as we shall see below) result in large-scale ethnic confrontations occurring instead of incipient class conflict (Levine 1976). Even where *wantok* groups are not in conflict with each other, their divergent rural foci and outside interests may fragment them (Rew 1974: 44).

We should stress again, as we did in the sections on *wantok* and ethnicity, that compatriotism creates a basis for the formation of urban social networks which are much more inclusive than rural ones, and as such are fundamental to the creation of wider loyalties and associational patterns in the towns. But since these are characteristically ethnically based, their influence on the development of *class* consciousness is divisive, as competition along ethnic lines cross-cuts or blurs competition and solidarity on socio-economic grounds.

This is not, however, the only set of forces undermining class formation. We have already mentioned that a rural orientation in itself may lessen active ideological commitment to the world of work. This leads to an unstable work-force which is difficult to organize. Rural–urban circulation, employment shifts, and a reluctance to acknowledge occupational differentiation as stratification also make any sustained leadership or organization among the workers highly problematic. Developmental factors, e.g. the low level of industrialization, and the lack of a comprehensive and coercive industrial framework such as was present on the African Copperbelt (Epstein 1958), tend to fragment most urban Papua New Guinean employees between different companies and various sectors of the economy where they face diverse specific problems. This is important, especially where Papua New Guineans attempt to create dyadic ties with their supervisors, treating the work relationship as reciprocal. Poor conditions become personal slights, not general aspects of one's class position. Finally, the low level of literacy, recency of substantial urbanization, lack of familiarity with idioms of industrial relations, and cultural heterogeneity, further discourage the emergence of class consciousness.

Although it is fair to say that class solidarity has not yet developed into a dominant theme in urban Papua New Guinea, the forces of worker fragmentation are counterbalanced to a degree by other factors. We have mentioned in the preceding pages that low pay, poor working conditions, discriminatory pay rates, etc., create great discontent. In many instances Papua New Guineans have united across ethnic lines to take industrial (class-oriented) action and have actually gone on strike. The pattern of these stoppages presents an elegant crystallization of the contradictory forces at work in the wider class arena.

From the reports of two researchers who have done studies of workers, stoppages appear to be spontaneous. One, which occurred at the company studied by Rew (1974: 199–206), started during a wave of strikes which hit Port Moresby in late 1965 and early 1966. Workers in the company had not played an active part in industrial affairs prior to the strike and management seemed genuinely surprised when 98 employees out of 120 decided to stop work one day late in 1965. Most of the day shift refused to start up and the entire night shift walked off the job. In the morning, the men began walking towards Koki market and were met on the road by Department of Labour and union officials. 'Wandering off to the market they appeared like lost sheep, unsure of where to go or what to do next' (ibid.: 200). They were persuaded to choose some representatives (six was the number suggested) for a conference between the parties relevant to the dispute. The men had made no prior complaints, were unsure of themselves and their grievances, raised issues that had little to do with the company and, aside from expressing discontent, achieved little in the end.

It seems that an important spur to their stoppage was a well-publicized action by administration drivers which had gained a great deal of attention in the town. Two Kerema men at the plant had kin at the transport pool and were kept informed of developments there. When word of another strike reached the compound, a group of mainly Kerema senior workers began to meet informally and decided to strike. The links used to gain further support included kinship and *wantok* ties, co-residence and common employment. No one person appeared especially instrumental as an organizer. Many men said they 'had simply joined groups of *wantok* who had discussed striking' (ibid.: 201). Although bonds of solidarity arose on the basis of being employees 'in the enthusiasm of the event', Rew stresses that these seemed much less significant than those which already existed in the plant. Conspicuously absent were groupings based on a system of representation throughout the plant or any industrial leadership units. The workers' bitterness, their like interests and sense of grievance was clear, 'but they lacked organization or coherence'. There was no list of demands, no leaders to present them or co-ordinate activity, and all the men were back on the job less than three hours later.

A strike reported from Madang (Stevenson 1968: 124–7) had a similar fate. Initial unity faded quickly and workers decided to return when faced with employer opposition. Action foundered here also because of a lack of clear leaders and the dependence on particularistic bonds among the workers.

Both of these accounts showed that the workers resented not only poor pay and conditions but the overall racial situation existing in the towns at the time. Although this may have led the men to make demands that employers could, with justification, dismiss as having nothing to do with their actual jobs, their desire for a new and more egalitarian social order was plain. However, as Stevenson points out, although the men share a common feeling of deprivation and antagonism towards employers, and have engaged in wildcat strikes, 'the cohesion between labourers finds no special ideological expression or justification' (ibid.: 127). Class solidarity was realized only temporarily in both strikes and collapsed quickly in the face of shows of strength by employers.

Although this may be the current state of class formation for unskilled workers, it seems that the semi-skilled or skilled and educated people are more involved in their class position. According to Whiteman (1973), as we mentioned before, the highly educated Chimbu are apt to evaluate even other Chimbu in class terms. M. Strathern (1975) also said that skilled Hageners are more aware of the class hierarchy than others. In the town as a whole the skilled are highly valued and in inter-ethnic contacts are accorded high prestige relative to unskilled people. They tend to feel they will stay in town longer than the unskilled. A number of our well-educated informants even confessed to great physical discomfort when they returned to village living conditions after having lived in town. With the expansion of localization and tertiary education, the numbers of such individuals are increasing rapidly. Unfortunately, in the absence of any in-depth study of the local élite that could shed more light for us on their class consciousness, we have only these bits and pieces of data from the relevant parts of the studies cited above. However, evidence suggests that their class position fundamentally affects their social lives and results in a substantial widening of their sphere of primary relationships.

Socio-economic position and primary ties

Research which has concentrated on a particular ethnic or tribal group in the local urban milieu (e.g. those discussed in the previous chapter) gives one the impression that primary ties with other Papua New Guineans are either non-existent or rather idiosyncratically made. Ryan says that even though the Toaripi had been living in Port Moresby for ten years at the time of her study, they had few contacts with people of other cultural or linguistic groups. Even those living outside Toaripi settlements (in government housing) are said to have little to do with their neighbours. She attributes this to the large number of Toaripi in Moresby. 'Indeed the number of migrants is so large that most people are able to associate almost exclusively with those who come from the same cluster of villages' (1968: 63). However, even in Lae, where there are considerably fewer of them, the Toaripi still keep relationships restricted to within the language group. The Buang in Lae appear fairly similar. As we mentioned in the previous chapter, Zimmerman characterizes these people as being almost completely isolated from non-Buangs in virtually every sphere of social life (1973: 89–91). Some scholars who do mention cross-ethnic friendships appear to see them as matters of individual circumstance. Oram (1967: 34) mentions that some Hula canoe settlement dwellers in the Koki area of Port Moresby have befriended New Guineans (mostly Highlanders) whom they met walking along the beach. He attributes these relationships to the loneliness of young Highlands men, whose overtures are accepted because the canoe dwellers gain material advantage and prestige from the relationships.

Strathern (M. Strathern 1975: 256) and Rew (1974) both mention that cross-ethnic relationships (mostly formed between co-workers, particularly if they share barracks quarters) are a measure of sophistication in the eyes of townsmen. The Hagener who feels himself belonging to the town and stresses his enjoyment of urban life, will often emphasize his network of non-Hagen friends. This is seen by Strathern as another instance of the stress on independence mentioned above. Most of these particular cross-ethnic ties appear to be rather superficial. Close relations with others are perceived as threatening to ethnic solidarity. It is to fellow Hageners that a man turns in times of trouble (M. Strathern 1975:164–6, 256–7).

Part of the tendency of some writers to stress the sparsity of inter-ethnic contacts and to minimize their importance may derive from the fact that the groups studied by urban anthropologists have often been ethnically defined and are composed of mainly unskilled labourers. In studying a particular ethnic group in town one tends to focus on mainly those occasions when people from that group are interacting. The common lack of attention to élites, even where élite members of the particular ethnic group are resident in the town, makes it difficult to control for socio-economic position in assessing the extent to which urban factors may influence such social relationships. This is an important question, however, as urbanization is often said to increase the scale and range of social interaction. We have, of course, been stressing this in our analysis of rurally derived or oriented social idioms. But it is the field of non-ethnic social relationships that is perhaps most distinctly urban, as they not only are formed in the towns and conditioned by urban events but may also operate without idioms of rural commonality. As such they are an aspect of participation in the wider urban sphere that would be particularly likely to be influenced by status in the urban system.

Some evidence to support this assertion comes from Whiteman, who divided the twenty families in her study on Chimbu social networks in Port Moresby into three categories: unsophisticated, semi-sophisticated and sophisticated. The sophisticated families had the most non-Chimbu in their social networks, and were more selective in their transactions with kin, avoiding social relationships with casual kin as much as possible. The unsophisticated families were the most encapsulated in Chimbu relationships (1973: 78–9, 86, 95, 101). If this pattern generally holds, socio-economic position and the spreading of social ties are positively related. It appears that such an uneven widening of ties may in itself contribute to a growing awareness of socio-economic differentiation on the part of urban Chimbu. According to Whiteman, her unskilled informants felt suspicious of skilled Chimbu whom they did not know well. This was because their style of life and activities set the skilled apart, but their contacts with non-Chimbu are said to be a contributing factor (ibid.: 44). Perhaps their participation in relationships with other ethnics is perceived as a sign of the emergence of new and divergent interests. With the added possibility, suggested by M. Strathern (1975), that people who favour urban life-styles stress such ties, we may be witnessing fundamental effects of socio-economic position on social relationships and a commitment to an urban style of life which will eventually solidify an as yet uncertain class consciousness.

Unfortunately, as is usual in in-depth network analysis, Whiteman's discussion of non-ethnic ties was based on a very small sample (there were only three sophisticated and four semi-sophisticated families) and is not an adequate base from which to generalize about inter-ethnic interaction patterns. Levine (1976) has, however, provided data from structured interviews of 212 informants from Mount Hagen (simple random sample), and 644 from Port Moresby (stratified random sample), which allow us to discern certain general trends in the formation of cross-ethnic primary ties.

This survey was designed to elicit information about participation with co-ethnics and non-ethnics in urban leisure time pursuits (drinking in bars, going to movies), and also enquired about which ethnic categories respondents' 'good friends' belonged to. As such, it was concerned only with the range of informants' contacts. More in-depth interviews with a much smaller and non-random sample of informants were carried out to supplement the larger survey with information about numbers of friends and their characteristics.

The results showed that formal education and participation in higher positions in the urban economy were associated with a greater range of inter-ethnic interaction. Unskilled workers had a wider range of inter-ethnic interaction than the unemployed, but much narrower than skilled and professional workers. When the results were broken down by residential area, the effect of education and employment differences between them was quite clear. Settlement dwellers from the Highlands interacted within a smaller ethnic range than did settlers from Papua or people living in urban resettlement areas which are more mixed. Low-covenant housing residents interacted with a very wide range, only exceeded by people living in university dormitories, police and army barracks. The only residential area which did not show the expected correlation between relatively high education and relatively wide interactive range was the one urban village sampled, Hanuabada in Port Moresby. This is perhaps because Hanuabadans inhabit an environment in which a full range of kinsmen with a diverse occupational background are neighbours.

When the results were examined with respect to other criteria, interesting but rather consistent results emerged. People from regions which were opened earliest, and who therefore had more formal education and better jobs, reported a relatively wide range of interaction. Highlanders were the most encapsulated in terms of inter-ethnic primary interaction, while people from the New Guinea Islands and Papua had more ethnically diverse friendship networks. Those few Highlanders living in low-covenant housing (who have relatively high educations) had a similar range of inter-ethnic interaction to the other residents. Women, who tend to be newer and more marginal urbanites than men, have consistently narrower inter-ethnic friendship networks than males except when they are more educated. University women, for example, have much wider networks than unskilled men.

In general the survey results indicated that greater participation in higher levels of the urban socio-economic hierarchy resulted in friendships with a more heterogeneous group of people. An in-depth look at individual informants' networks showed that other ethnics in the friendship network were almost always of the same objective class position as the informant and had common job and other interests. Cross-status ties, on the other hand, were almost always mono-ethnic. The patterns were so consistent that the effect of socio-economic status and related variables on a widening of cross-ethnic friendships seems indisputable. The more socio-economically marginal tend to be segregated from others spatially in discrete settlements and socially in terms of friendships. For Highlanders, for example, this means they have a greater distance from other urbanites than do members of other regions. This distance is associated with ignorance, fear and the projection of stereotypes on to them by others.

Despite the clarity of the relationship between an individual's socio-economic position and the ethnic range of his friendships, the fact remains that skilled and educated informants do maintain close contacts with less well-placed fellow ethnics, playing down these differences during their interaction. On the other hand, it is likely that high-status urbanites are becoming less involved with fellow ethnics as a result of their 'branching out' (which would only be logical since every inter-ethnic friendship limits the time one can spend with co-ethnics). But whatever the effect of objective class on interactional patterns, their influence on subjective class consciousness remains uncertain. It is possible that differentiation of life-style, activities and friendship patterns will eventually result in a weakening of ethnic (but not close kinship) social ties for the well educated, while the unskilled remain more 'ethnic' than class conscious, at least partially because of their high degree of escapsulation. For the present, however, the relevance of ethnicity is great for all urbanites.

Ethnicity in the wider urban field

A number of scholars have recognized that ethnicity may have greater power to determine allegiance than class. Class ties have strength or potential because they derive from common interests which may become effective bases for collective action, while 'Ethnicity has become more salient because it can combine an interest with an affective tie' (Bell 1975: 169). It provides sets of common identifications while other social roles may be more abstract and impersonal (ibid.). Ethnicity can also serve to mobilize large groups in the course of struggles for political and economic power in established and new states. Accordingly, now that the departure of the colonial power has led to competition between Papua New Guineans for control of scarce political and economic resources, it has largely been pursued along ethnic lines, as 'regional development' continues to be a dominant, high-level political theme.

When we discussed ethnicity as a basis of primary relations in the last chapter, a number of factors that encouraged the emergence of wider than traditional identities were mentioned. A classificatory system of ethnic labels based on colonial divisions, uneven rural development and stereotypes modelled on these, and the pursuance of disputes as group matters, were said to be factors that entered into social relations, encouraging the assumption of higher-level identities. When we add to these the element of competition in regional and national arenas, the identities tend to become even wider. In a new state, where lines of conflict and co-operation are still being worked out, the mobilization of identities may shift with different issues and areas. Because the identities' dimensions are set by colonial and national political boundaries, the participants may try to make these more meaningful by defining their mutual differences and similarities in terms of behavioural stereotypes. Although particular development issues tend to be specific to the different centres, ethnic stereotypes are more generally salient, so we will begin our discussion of ethnicity in the wider urban field with an account of some common urban stereotypes before going on to illustrations of ethnic formations in selected towns.

Stereotypes

We have noted that common ethnic stereotypes are phrased in terms of colonial and national administrative divisions. The perception of the stereotyped categories as true groups by urbanites helps to reinforce the salience of these essentially artificial boundaries in the creation of more general ethnic units that are emerging in the towns. The entrance of these stereotypes into everyday life interactional situations as part of a common set of urban cultural expectations helps structure inter-ethnic encounters and indicates a strong and pervasive potential base for group formation.

Before we go on to discuss some of the stereotypes that are commonly used in a variety of towns, we should point out that there exist lower-level ones that operate in specific centres or regions but that rarely extend beyond them. In Mount Hagen, for example, certain proclivities are commonly said to characterize local Melpa speakers such as violence, theft and big-headedness. In Port Moresby, however, Hageners as such have no particular reputation, being subsumed under the category of 'Highlanders' and tagged with that stereotype. On the other hand, Goilalas in Port Moresby are noted for fierceness and often blamed for murders. But informants living in Mount Hagen, who had not been to Port Moresby and had never heard of Goilalas, would categorize them (and any other Central Province dwellers) as Papuans, who have quite a different sort of reputation. In every urban area ideas about specific traditional groups may be held by local people which are much less relevant in other towns. Although these are interesting and part of the sociology of the various towns, their variety and specificity makes a full consideration of them impossible here.

With respect to the more common stereotypes, the distinction between Papua and New Guinea is fundamental. The regions of Papua, the Highlands, the Islands and New Guinea Coast are also important. When stereotypes are cast in such terms, two are usually counterposed: Highlanders speak of themselves in contrast to people from lowland areas or 'Coastals', Papua contrasts with New Guinea, and the Islands with the mainland.

The recent influx of Highlanders into most large towns, in the marginal positions detailed in earlier chapters, has created a rather pervasive tendency for people from other parts of the country to label them as 'primitive'. *Bus kanaka*, perhaps the most derogatory terms of abuse which can be directed towards New Guineans, means just that. Because of news reports concerning tribal fighting in their region, and the sometimes unruly behaviour of young urban Highlanders (who are less likely than other Papua New Guineans to have families with them in town), they are also often said to be violent.

The Highlands stereotype is not entirely negative however. The enthusiasm with which the region approaches cash-cropping, the high production of tea and coffee, and the building of the Highlands Highway with largely local labour, gives Highlanders the valued image of being a hardworking people with great initiative for rural business. A reputation for political conservatism flowing from their general opposition to early self-government and independence fill out the content of the stereotype.

The violent image of Highlanders in Bougainville's towns, and the murder of two prominent Bougainvillean public servants in Goroka in 1973, helped to solidify calls for that island's secession from the rest of Papua New Guinea. Bougainville, far from the mainland centres, was relatively neglected until huge copper deposits were uncovered there and exploited by foreign interests. The copper company's presence resulted in dislocations and possibilities for wealth for the island which caused considerable ambivalence towards the project. Much of the proceeds from the mine go to foreign countries in the form of profits, and as taxes to the distant government in Port Moresby. In addition, a large demand for outside workers prompted the arrival of many 'foreigners' to the island and, as we have seen, its towns have a most unbalanced demography and unstable urban population. All these factors, plus the darkness of Bougainvilleans' skin which easily differentiates them from mainlanders, contributed to their declared secession from Papua New Guinea soon after independence. This breakaway was not officially recognized, however, and the rift seems to be healing now that new promises of greater provincial autonomy have been made in Port Moresby.

A survey of schools in and near south Bougainville's towns (Mamak and Bedford 1974) found that students were unfavourably disposed towards New Guineans, citing drinking, physical violence, fights, killings and sexual incidents as reasons for their antipathy. The students often qualified their statements by saying that it was the unskilled or unemployed who were causing the trouble. Good New Guineans were skilled Coastals, bad ones were 'Chimbu' (i.e. Highlands) 'drain diggers'. But the fear of New Guineans (mainlanders) became generalized in the context of nationalistic statements and, according to Mamak and Bedford, Bougainvilleans were rapidly becoming convinced of a need for unity and defence in the face of changing conditions. Their consciousness was fundamentally affected by the presence of urban migrants in their midst. As one man said, 'Niugineans say we want secession because copper is on our land. This is not true; the truth is that whenever we have worked with them ... and there is a fight they turn round and call us "black bastards"' (ibid.: 12).

Such negative images of and reactions against migrants (especially Highlanders) have also been used to articulate regionalism in other centres. Coastals in Highlands towns feel vulnerable to attack and their fellows in coastal centres see lawlessness as a product of the migration of unskilled inland workers. Highlanders for their part react against such charges by stressing the positive contribution their labour has made to the country's economy and the face of its towns. They criticize Coastals (especially Papuans) for their reputed laziness and political opportunism. Highlanders greatly resent Coastals' socio-economic dominance and get especially angry with statements that they (Highlanders) should be sent home from the towns which they feel that they built with their own muscle.

In Port Moresby the rise of Papua Besena (also a secessionist movement) was helped by the articulation of New Guinean stereotypes which were quite similar to those encountered in Bougainville. These were combined with grievances relating to the underdevelopment of Papua as a whole. Allusions on the part of the movement's leader to the cold 'wind from the mountains' which woke Papuans up from the long sleep that colonialism had lulled them into, and references to the placing of foxes among sheep, could hardly be missed as verbal attacks on violent New Guineans, again especially Highlanders. In Rabaul, where many Highland plantation labourers are found, similar feelings are also expressed, as well as resentment for recent government neglect of that area's problems (Levine 1976).

On an everyday level, these stereotypes of Highlanders, New Guineans and Coastals, which reflect their relative incorporation into the towns and the nation, primarily operate on informal levels and, as mentioned above, enter into ethnic encounters, rumours, gossip, etc. They serve to delineate *potential* bases of support. Thus people remain conscious of their ability to use the categories that these stereotypes refer to in the course of high-level confrontations or as appeals to solidarity in a variety of specific situations. They encourage individuals to become more ethnic than class conscious: urbanites are amenable to appeals based on general ethnicity as these combine affective, political and economic elements.

Mobilizing such categories into groups for purposes of competition in developing political arenas is a difficult task despite its facilitation by the prevalence of such stereotypes. The stereotypes provide elements of form and content and also delineate areas of relative friendship network density (Levine 1976). Nevertheless, the categories' high level masks internal difficulties and schisms that sometimes take precedence. Being situational, they are only likely to become truly consistent bases of identification when disputes regularize and persist. Even then, a certain amount of formal organization is needed to create effective ethnic co-alitions out of these broad categories. At present most wider ethnic alignments are in the process of becoming more regularized, but substantial impediments to their consistent mobilization exist in all centres. An idea of the present state of ethnicity as a basis of collective action can be gained by an examination of the development of ethnic amalgamation in those towns (other than the Bougainville case mentioned above) for which we have detailed information.

Some examples of ethnic polarization in the wider urban field

General factors contributing to current urban ethnic amalgamation in Papua New Guinea are by no means peculiar to that country. As is true of other topics discussed in this monograph, the specific constellations of local factors which combine to produce unique situations have their parallels throughout the developing (and developed) world. In India, for example, the sorts of ethnic coalitions we discuss here form around, and are expressed through, 'language demands'. Language is used as a marker for delineating collectivities which compete for power and resources in India's national political arena (Das Gupta 1975). Although in Papua New Guinea issues tend to articulate along regional or sub-regional lines more often than language, the fate of ethnic amalgamations in both countries (and many others as well) reflects 'how these transformations are worked out in particular contexts of resource, culture, rules, organization and statemanship'. Specific definitions of the collectivity to be mobilized, the way it is organized, its interaction with other groups and the nature of local politics (ibid.: 469, 488) substantially determine whether the categories remain relevant only in the realm of personal relationships and interactions or become bases for effective collective action.

Ethnic coalitions in three towns, Mount Hagen, Rabaul and Port Moresby, illustrate the way in which these factors and their effects on the course of ethnic amalgamation vary in Papua New Guinea's towns and their hinterlands. In each urban area inclusive local identities, 'Hagen', 'Tolai' and 'Papuan', have formed in contradistinction to urban migrants who are represented as competitors for jobs, and fomenters of urban and peri-urban trouble. Fights, road accidents, thefts, drunkenness and sexual assaults or advances by male migrants usually take precedence in everyday situations as foci for individual grievance. The element of competition for urban resources remains strong, however, especially because urban expansion requires the alienation of land belonging to the local group. This encourages peri-urban tribesmen to view the town as theirs, or at least to argue that more of its services and opportunities should be directed towards them.

Of the three identities, Hagen and Tolai are on essentially the same level of inclusiveness, while Papuan (in Port Moresby) is obviously a considerably wider referent of identification. Despite similarities in both the scale of Hagen and Tolai identities and in the current issues affecting their expression, the former provides a much weaker basis for sustained organization than the latter. The factors affecting the relative inclusiveness and strength of these identities and their effectiveness as bases of collective organization are epiphenomena of specific local aspects of colonization and the transition to independence (together with factors mentioned in previous sections).

Particularly relevant to collective organization in each case are the date and policies of various colonial regimes, the quality of the land and amount which was alienated, the density of the autochthonous population, the size of the towns, the small-scale nature of traditional indigenous societies, and present processes of change in the towns' hinterlands. As these cases help show, urbanization is part of a more general series of social changes which are occurring in Papua New Guinea, all of which influence each other. Although ethnic coalitions are important urban social forms in each area, their referents importantly include rural problems and political aspirations. Some appreciation of rural social change is therefore necessary to an understanding of the generation of these coalitions.

Rabaul

At the time of initial contact the Tolai of the Gazelle Peninsula, East New Britain, were divided into many separate and often warring social groups. Although there was a degree of cultural commonality and common participation in shared socio-cultural institutions (shell money, religion and cults), there was no common Tolai name nor 'historical tradition' (Epstein 1970: 155–72).

A number of factors are seen by Epstein as influencing the growth of a Tolai identity. The use of the label 'Tolai' to designate people from the Gazelle was probably first employed by Papuans and other New Guineans 'working alongside Tolai at Edie Creek and Bulolo gold mines in the early 1930s' and 'became accepted by the people themselves'. Since the Gazelle was colonized earlier than other areas, its residents had a head start over other indigenes in their education and began to look upon themselves as an élite (ibid.). In addition, land alienation, population growth, heavy involvement in cash-cropping, resultant land pressures, and the limited capacity of the town of Rabaul to absorb Tolai workers, have greatly influenced the development of new oppositions and solidarities in the Gazelle, encouraging the growth of a strong Tolai identity.

Mount Hagen

The factors described above as lying behind the development of a Tolai ethnic coalition are not peculiar to Rabaul. For the Mount Hagen area we have a similar degree of pre-contact cultural similarity, and the *moka* ceremonial exchange system (A. J. Strathern 1971) seems to have created a degree of interdependence similar to that reported for pre-contact Tolai. Land has been alienated for expatriate plantations, the town and administrative projects. Although this has been less than in the Tolai case, more land has been alienated in the Mount Hagen area than anywhere else in the Highlands. Hageners, like Tolai, are involved in significant cash-cropping and have a large and growing population. Both areas have been exposed to the same western educational, religious and political institutions and Mount Hagen town is similar in size to Rabaul (excluding urban villages). Like the Tolai, Hagens have seen a large number of outsiders placed within their midst, but these people came more recently, and in different colonial circumstances. Despite these similarities and the existence in both amalgamations of competing lower-level loyalties, the balance in the Hagen area is more on the side of relatively low-level identities, whereas introduced change in the Gazelle has led to a strong Tolai ethnic coalition. In order to appreciate this differential strength we will first look a little more deeply at general effects of western institutions in the Hagen hinterland, and then at the contrasting responses to national politics apparent in each area which demonstrates the comparative strength of the Tolai coalition.

According to A. J. Strathern (1974), endemic warfare existed in the Hagen area along with frequent ceremonials in which items of wealth (pigs and shells) were exchanged to initiate or restore amicable relations between groups. These *moka* exchanges also are vehicles of group competition as prestige and strength are expressed through superior prestations (A. J. Strathern 1971, 1974: 243). When government officials began coming to the Hagen area in the late 1930s, the shells, which traditionally could only be obtained via trade through a host of known and unknown intermediaries, were used as payment for labour, land and food. At the same time that these traditional wealth items were becoming more abundant, efforts were being made by administration officials to stop tribal fighting. The effect of these two factors was that more wealth enabled Hageners to hold festivals more often or more impressively than before (1974: 243). Thus they could create more friendships, and in lieu of warfare could continue fighting 'quite effectively in a ritualized medium' (ibid.). The *moka* system was thus strengthened, and 'group rivalries, cleavages, enmities, and alliances have all been maintained' (ibid.: 246).

Perhaps because the administration's presence was reinforcing traditional means of organization and bringing new opportunities as well, Hageners reacted to colonial domination with much less opposition than the Tolai. This, of course, has primary relevance to the fragility of urban Hagen ethnic coalitions. Furthermore, the introduction of local government councils into this environment has provided a niche for traditional political competition (ibid.: 248) and has resulted in far less political integration than in the Gazelle.

National elections and opposition to the administration in Rabaul and Mount Hagen

In this discussion of continuity and change in the hinterland of Mount Hagen and Rabaul, we are presented with a picture of relatively greater continuity in the former. This is well illustrated and perhaps better appreciated through a brief account of the 1968 House of Assembly elections, as well as a number of local incidents, which give a good indication of the way in which ethnic identities are phrased in the context of political issues and oppositions in each area.

Just before the elections in the Gazelle, a group of villagers occupied a section of the expatriate-owned Raniola plantation. They told plantation workers from other parts of the country to leave and then proceeded to plant their own crops. They were later forced off by the police. A leading part in the Raniola occupation was played by Oscar Tammur, a candidate in the 1968 campaign for Kokopo Open Electorate. The incumbent running for the other local seat, Mathias Toliman, supported the action strongly. Both won by comfortable majorities (Chowning, Epstein, Goodale and Grosart 1971: 53), illustrating the importance of land in the election, and the popular opposition to expatriate landowners and the colonial administration's efforts to protect their claims.

To the catalogue of points of local opposition to the administration, expatriates and migrant natives, was added the issue of a new factory at Ulapia which was said to be recruiting Sepiks instead of Tolai people. Considering the growing Tolai population, land shortage, and stagnation of Rabaul, the jobs were an important resource. Also, the administration decided that the expansion of school building in the Gazelle was to be slowed down in favour of other areas. This was a direct threat to the élite position of the Tolai in various fields of endeavour.

In 1974, serious riots occurred in the Rabaul–Kokopo area between plantation workers and autochthonous people. The immediate cause of the trouble was said to be an attempted sexual assault by a 'Chimbu' (Highlander) on a local girl. Although the plantation workers came from a number of Highlands and Sepik districts, they were able to unite in the context of fighting the Tolai, who of course co-operated with each other. This trouble with 'Highlanders' served to increase Tolai cohesion and sharpen their concern about the presence of so many urban and peri-urban migrants in their area. It is interesting to note that this incident, which has definite class overtones (the 'Highlanders' were not all from the Highlands, but were all plantation workers), was cast in ethnic terms, as a Highlander–Tolai confrontation, by all concerned.

The House of Assembly elections in the Hagen area present a different picture with a more pervasive concern with the importance of lower-level units. Most of the candidates were looking for support and campaigning on the basis of 'the segmentation of their electorates' (Colebatch, Colebatch, Reay and Strathern 1971: 219). Although this segmentation had a varying base, traditional and council politics (the latter being to a large degree also traditional) played a greater role than in the Tolai area.

Most candidates had been in the councils and traditional ideas concerning status played a large part in the election.

The administration and its officers also played a formidable role in the election process. The continuing atmosphere of paternalism in the Western Highlands makes a striking contrast with the situation in the Gazelle. When the Tolai were fighting against the administration, the Australian Western Highlands District Commissioner was being called '*God bilong mipela*' by local councillors referring to his proven power to develop the district. The District Commissioner himself was known to remind people in church that his authority over them was granted by God (ibid.: 222). Administration officers could easily influence people to run and directly affected the outcome of the Hagen elections (ibid.).

The overriding importance of oppositions between Hagens is well illustrated in accounts of difficulties in Mul–Dei electorate very near Hagen town. During the 1968 election campaigns, low-level inter-tribal and traditional style council disputes (which were sparked off by a series of incidents including a traffic fatality, a payback killing and many pervasive and conflicting rumours) resulted in an atmosphere of violence and fear. 'In such circumstances there was no possibility of vigorous cross-tribal campaigning,' and indeed the voting followed tribal lines (A. J. Strathern 1976: 274).

Thus the election contests in Hagen were waged in terms of lower-level identities than on the Gazelle. Particularly interesting was the relative lack of opposition between Hagens and outsiders. The kinds of issues present on the Gazelle in 1968 were not evident and disputes between Hagens themselves were most prominent.

These differences seem due primarily to the contrasting histories of colonization in Hagen and the Gazelle. Europeans were still rather awesome people to Hagens, but their presence was not overly disruptive of traditional modes of organization. Expatriate plantations were perceived more as models for business activities than as depriving Hagens of opportunities. As expansion of European presence was welcomed, land problems were less likely to be phrased in terms of 'Hagens' versus 'Europeans' and rather expressed in warfare between Hagens. Indeed, as colonization was fading, tribal fighting increased throughout the Highlands, being especially prevalent in the Mount Hagen area. Enmity between two peri-urban Hagen clans (the Jiga and Yamuga) has been traced to land pressure caused by the town's expansion. In Rabaul, on the other hand, the Tolai protested against administration seizure of land for public works from as early as 1935 in a case which reached the League of Nations Permanent Mandates Commission (Epstein 1969: 195). The relatively benevolent nature of Mount Hagen's more recent colonization, the lack of experience with western institutions, and a surge in economic development with the opening of the Highlands Highway seemed to encourage Hagens to see the colonial administration as powerful and working in the interests of desired development and change. Paternalism was the order of the day, and throughout this period Mount Hagen's growth brought more job opportunities as well as an increased demand for cash-crops and greater contacts with other groups.

This greater contact has increased the scope of groups with which disputes may arise, particularly in the case of vehicular accidents. When these involve outsiders (e.g. people from the Enga Province), pushes towards Hagen ethnic amalgamation become quite powerful (Levine 1976). But with Europeans bowing out and uncertainty about the future developing, Hageners (and other Highlanders) seem to be relying on traditional means of settling grievances and feel less afraid to fight since the autocratic ways of the strong *kiaps* (administration patrol officers) of the past have been replaced by more democratic administrative efforts involved with the transition to independence. Although contacts with other Highlanders and the influx of expatriates and other Papua New Guineans has led to a definite growth of an urban 'Hagen' ethnic co-alition, its importance seems less immediate than the lower-level iden-tities and antagonisms which the same processes of change have rein-forced.

Port Moresby

When we attempt to explain the significance of the higher-level Papua versus New Guinea opposition, and the emergence of a Papuan identity in Port Moresby, purely local cultural aggregations and hinterland politics become less central to the discussion, although they remain important. Many of the same factors that have been operating in the Gazelle have been at work to define Motu and Koita identity: the long history of colonization, pacification, the presence of outsiders, early council development, sophistication, land alienation by the government and (in this case) encroachment by migrants and squatters from other parts of Papua New Guinea and a common religious mission, have led to the importance of a wider identity (similar in scale to the Tolai identity) for Port Moresby's autochthonous population. This is particularly important in disputes over land with people from the Gulf Province which the administration is attempting to mediate.

However, the basic economic and historical factors which led to the growth of a region-wide Papuan identity have, because of the specific demographic and urban growth patterns of the Port Moresby area, more fundamentally affected the Motu and Koita in Port Moresby than New

Guinea (or Highlands) identity has affected Hagens and Tolais in their respective areas.

Because land was less productive in the Moresby region, the local indigenous population was small. Motu and Koita in and around the town number less than 7000. Alienation was not as strongly contested there as in Rabaul, though recently land has become valuable both as real estate and as underpinning for local identities. Whereas Mount Hagen and Rabaul are small regional centres, Port Moresby is a city of over 75,000. The urban population swamps the local indigenes in Port Moresby, unlike Mount Hagen and Rabaul where the opposite relationship holds. This is reflected in the absence of a feeling that Port Moresby is an island set in the midst of a powerful indigenous culture area. The town itself seems in certain superficial ways to have swallowed up its Motu and Koita inhabitants. Although their villages exist in its midst, there is little in their appearance that distinguishes them as traditional settlements. This is somewhat true of Rabaul as well, but whereas gardening remains very important to urban Tolai villagers, Port Moresby's autochthonous inhabitants gave up subsistence agriculture long ago (Belshaw 1957) and are mainly wage-earners. The demographic ratio of town to indigenes is such that Port Moresby can absorb the Motu and Koita as wage-earners (as well as numerous migrants), which gives it the atmosphere of a cosmopolitan Papuan town.

Despite the fact that Motu and Koita are significant identities in many contexts, they are bound to be relatively ineffective in others. The Tolai can oppose Highlanders, and Coastals and Europeans may fear Hagens, but the Motu and Koita are not in a similar position of potential strength in Port Moresby. In situations calling for opposition to a high-level category encompassing all or a large number of outsiders, organizing around Motu and Koita identities would be insufficient.

These aspects of the local situation which we have just discussed, the fact that Port Moresby is Papua's only significant town, its large Papuan population, and the recent large-scale migrations of New Guineans into the area, have made 'Papuan' an important Port Moresby identity. Although, as we have seen in a previous chapter, the basic division between Papua and New Guinea has reference and appeal in a wider context, it is in Port Moresby that the circumstances outlined above have led to a mobilization around Papuan identity expressed most forcibly in the growth of the Papua Besena movement, Papuan state agitation, and actual confrontations with New Guineans. Thus we have in Port Moresby the somewhat ironic situation of a secessionist movement dominating the city council of a new nation's capital and the development within it of a strong, nation-splitting identity.

Summary

The towns of Mount Hagen, Port Moresby and Rabaul are set within matrices of historical, economic, demographic, colonial and geographical factors which, though broadly similar, differ in particular aspects and overall combination for each town. A prevailing 'atmosphere' created in each area by the constellation of elements discussed above serves to direct ethnic choices more consistently towards certain levels of the ethnic hierarchy. The atmosphere in the Hagen area, which has led to a fragile Hagen identity, strengthens lower-level units and undermines the more inclusive Hagen coalition. Although Tolai and Papuan amalgamations are also subject to fissiparous pressures, historical events and present realities have more consistently reinforced their importance than in the Hagen case. Unlike the former, Papuan and Tolai ethnic coalitions show more than passing durability and have led to the growth of strong and well-organized political movements capable of pursuing various Papuan and Tolai interests and goals in national political arenas. Of the two more solid ethnic coalitions, the Tolai one is probably the more durable. Active Tolai political groups formed more quickly than did their counterparts in Papua; and Gazelle secessionism, plantation take-overs and the assassination of a colonial official all took place prior to Papuan activism. The Tolai Mataungan Association (formed in 1969 to oppose Australian attempts to include expatriates in the Gazelle Local Government Council) is an important part of the present coalition government. Land pressure in the Gazelle, the nature of their colonial experience and the greater socio-cultural similarity of the Tolai are all factors in the relative strength of that ethnic coalition.

Conclusion

In this chapter we have tried to demonstrate that the objective conditions of Papua New Guinean urbanization discussed in previous chapters and social idioms developed by urbanites in the course of establishing bases of personal security, have continued to influence the course of adaptation, interaction and socio-cultural categorization in the wider urban field. The creative and flexible employment of rural social idioms and styles by the urban population is becoming the predominant force behind Papua New Guinean urban social organization. A muting of the salience of growing class divisions, and the development of wider ethnic loyalties which become foci of schism and dispute, are dominant urban social themes which we have shown to be epiphenomena of colonial history, objective urban conditions and rural social forms.

Of these emergent ethnic amalgamations, Tolais and Papuans have had the greatest impact on urban and national arenas, stemming from their development of formal associations (Mataungans and Papua Besena), which are capable of sustained political mobilization. Although they do have a certain impact on urban life as organizations, Papua Besena and the Mataungans are regionally oriented groups not concerned with furthering the needs of urbanites *per se*. The achievement of some specifically urban-oriented goals and aspirations (e.g. the desire for better working conditions or the acquisition of substantial business capital) may, however, be greatly facilitated by the development of voluntary organizations which operate not only on a wider than traditional scale, but along formally constituted lines which provide structural and procedural avenues towards the accomplishment of specific tasks by such wider groupings. Performing in a formal organizational milieu and dealing with western-style bureaucratic agencies are aspects of urbanization which will increasingly affect Papua New Guineans as they operate in the wider urban field. It is to this aspect of urbanization that we now turn.

6. Formal institutions in the wider urban field

Although Papua New Guineans have transformed the social and cultural life of their nation's towns, it is important to emphasize that they do not as yet make a substantial input into the decision-making processes of those institutions that are responsible for the administration of urban affairs. The bureaucracy that controls such important functions as town planning, education, the police and the courts, as well as the provision of water, sewage and innumerable permits and licences (for building, businesses, etc.), is remote and alien to the man in the street. Despite the fact that the nation is independent and a government elected by the people has control over all aspects of administration, the administrative forms remain colonial in style and operation. This provides substantial obstacles to urbanites who, when not actually hindered, are certainly not helped in their adjustment to urban life by the maze of red tape and regulations that, for example, prevents them from setting up a small business (Fitzpatrick and Blaxter 1976) and complicates the procedure of getting water supplied to their settlements. Contacts with the administration are often frustrating (as when an illiterate man has to apply for a block of land or a dog licence on the proper form, in duplicate, complete with small print) and sometimes downright hostile. The procedures or verdicts of the courts and permit-granting bodies are seldom understood, while the police, garrisoned in barracks separate from the rest of the urban population, are looked upon as invaders when they go into the settlements to search for 'vagrants' or stolen property.

People (understandably) try to avoid the administration when they can, but by doing so they allow it to continue to affect their lives in many ways. The lack of a suitable framework for the constructive and co-operative involvement of townsmen in urban government seriously impedes the fuller 'Melanesianization' and social integration of the urban areas. This state of affairs is attributable not only to the western styles of organization, laws and procedures which permeate the town's formal institutions, but also to the disorganization of the urban administrative apparatus itself, which was inherited from a colonial authority notable for its reluctance to allow natives into towns for more than short periods (Oram 1976). In addition, townsmen have not been successful in their efforts to organize effective lobbying mechanisms to press for change in both government and private sectors.

In this chapter we will explore the gap between urbanites and urban institutions (which has been given little prominence in the local literature) through discussions of the urban bureaucracy, indigenous voluntary associations, and the interactions between one group of local people (urban businessmen) and government departments.

Urban administration

It was only in 1971 that town councils, the central bodies responsible for the unified administration of urban areas, began to be set up in Port Moresby, Lae and Madang. The state of urban government prior to that has been characterized by Oram (1972) as disorganized. He maintains that the dislike of native urbanization manifested by the colonial government (as well as by Papua New Guinea's present leaders) has led to administrative inertia which is reflected in a lack of bureaucratic co-ordination and responsiveness and in the adoption of unrealistic policies, especially in regard to land and housing (Oram 1976: 237–40). As we have seen in Chapter Two, the lack of a positive approach to housing has largely segregated the urban population on an ethnic basis. Although a clustering of urbanites by area of origin occurs in many towns (for a variety of reasons), Oram maintains that the policies of the Papua New Guinea administration has led to a greater social isolation than exists in the towns of other developing nations (ibid.: 240). He argues that a reorganization is needed and that local urbanites, if given opportunities for participation in urban government, may by co-operating with one another overcome feelings of alienation from the wider urban field and begin to solve some of the town's emerging social problems.

The disorganization of the bureaucracy itself stemmed from the fact that the Australians developed institutions for dealing with a rural native population and continued using them in relation to indigenous urbanites. No comprehensive urban legislation was formulated and there was no co-ordination of those aspects of the various government departments and agencies which related to urban areas. Towns were administered as part of sub-districts and were not provided with a separate governmental apparatus. Decisions in some larger towns were made directly by central government departments (e.g. Health, Lands and Surveys, etc.) without the knowledge of district commissioners who were in any case more used to dealing with villagers than urbanites. Revenue for those operations that were carried out in urban areas came from the central government and the tax framework did not allow for independent urban councils. Although the colonial government set up rural local government councils giving villagers a certain amount of control over very local level developments, the inclusion of the indigenous urban population in some of these was restricted to those people who were living on native land (only about 20 per cent of the population of Port Moresby, for example). Other urbanites were left without representation on any specifically urban body. In sum, administrative disorganization resulted in a rather incomprehensible and arbitrary bureaucracy with no channels to the people, and only haphazard and ineffectual attempts to provide a viable framework for urban government. Urban problems could not be viewed in their wider perspective by the various central government departments, and urbanites were left basically to their own devices (Oram 1972, 1976: 209–16). Although this has had the positive effect of encouraging Papua New Guineans to provide their own solutions to their problems, enabling them to use their own socio-cultural idioms and connections to the fullest extent possible, it is clear that a mechanism which has meaning and coherence for the Papua New Guineans is needed to bring them together to the task of creating solid national centres out of the hollow and segmented towns they now occupy.

Steps have been taken to remove administration from the district office to urban councils in some towns, but only Port Moresby's council has been studied in detail and its fate seems to hang very much in the balance (Oram 1976: 221–60). The Port Moresby City Council, established in 1971, was given power over tax collection, minor public works, parks and community centres, illegal buildings and rubbish collection, as well as a mandate to advise on the problems and needs of the residents of the council's seven wards. Although ward committees have been formed and began to meet regularly in most areas, the council faces a severe shortage of well-trained staff with which to interdigitate effectively the workings of the council with the needs of local urbanites. Because the central government continues to work independently of the council in Port Moresby, there still remains a lack of co-ordination of urban government organizations. The council is cut off from the people on the one hand and from the central government on the other. Unless it can establish effective links with both, its potential as an integrative device will not be actualized.

The inefficiency and administrative chaos stressed above has meant that no viable structure of formal organizational integration has been presented to urban Papua New Guineans. They, on the other hand, have not effectively organized themselves in such a way as to be able to press for the creation of more responsive and participatory bodies to deal with government and the private sector. We mentioned in the last chapter that the success of the Mataungan and Papua Besena movements was due to their ability to organize on formal lines to maintain a sustained wider political mobilization. If Papua New Guineans could develop and use such organizations for urban purposes they would perhaps be in a position either to take over aspects of urban administration themselves or to co-operate more fully in the processes of setting up a viable organizational structure. To appreciate the current status of attempts in this direction we turn to a consideration of local voluntary associations.

Voluntary associations

The role of ethnic or regional associations is central to the social life of towns in many developing areas, as reports from Asia, Africa and Latin America indicate (e.g. Doughty 1970, Fallers 1967, Little 1957). Gugler, for example, maintains that ethnic associations constitute 'the most prevalent type of groups characterized by intensive participation on the urban scene in sub-Saharan Africa today. They condition the identification of their members, shape their interaction, articulate their interests – both in the urban environment and for their rural homes' (1975: 301). He also notes that specific ethnic associations frequently amalgamate into district- or province-wide bodies in order to exert pressure more effectively on local administrations. These intricate and multi-functional organizations are so effective in controlling urban migrants that they have had various functions of urban administration delegated to them (such as tax collection and justice) in various towns. Such associations provide experience in bureaucratic leadership and organization that serves members well when they seek to enter politics or business (ibid.: 299–307). These institutions seem to provide mechanisms whereby urbanites in other nations have achieved a fair degree of power and direct influence in the wider urban field. Their development in Papua New Guinea would perhaps herald the attainment of fuller adaptation and the beginnings of true control of their new environments by the nation's urbanites.

It is certainly apparent that the ethnic base and the framework for wider ethnic amalgamation exists in urban Papua New Guinea. But despite the existence of a considerable number and variety of voluntary associations in the larger towns, the role of such organizations in the urbanization process seems slight in comparison with that reported from other developing areas (Oeser 1969: 40–1, 114, Oram 1976: .142, Rew 1974: 29). Church groups and sporting clubs, often having active and committed indigenous members, are an exception to this rule.

Mekeo migrants working in Port Moresby organized the Mekeo Sports Club for the purpose of playing rugby – against a similar Mekeo migrant team based in Lae – during the Christmas season, when most members of both groups would be back home on holiday leave (Rew 1974: 61–3). This team was eventually expanded into two teams which became involved in the regular Junior League competitions in Port Moresby. The supporters came from many different Mekeo villages, but included a number of 'marginally-Mekeo' recruits, as well as non-Mekeos (from the Marshall Lagoon area of the Central District) introduced by a Mekeo who had married a woman from that area. The club's affairs went smoothly and it successfully survived its dynamic first president's transferral to another town. The Mekeos themselves seemed to feel that the sports club was the making of their community in Port Moresby, providing their several 'small mutually suspicious groups' of clansmen and friends with 'a collective solidarity they had never previously experienced' (1974: 61–3).

As migrants from particular areas came to specific towns their respective missions began providing pastors and facilities for them in the urban areas. Since various denominations tend to be associated with specific rural spheres of influence, urban church membership is often regionally based (Oram 1976: 137). This of course helps to further reinforce ethnic loyalties in the towns (Lucas 1972: 267–8, Oram 1976: 138).

Urban churches typically become foci for the development of youth groups and women's clubs and may also be involved in running hostels. The Port Moresby Community Development Group, which trains indigenous social workers to aid the organization of urban settlement committees, is funded and directed by a number of churches. The relative success of urban church groups no doubt stems from the long history of missionary organizations in Papua New Guinea. The fact that they were the first western-style institutions to deal with large numbers of local people, converting them to active participation long before urban migration began, made it fairly easy for church organizations to set up congregations in towns, especially if influential elders became urban migrants. Committed expatriates either established or ran church affairs, or (more recently) have trained local people to assume leadership positions over a number of years. Although urban churches may be important to the social lives of local villagers and others from relatively close hinterland areas, many people migrating to towns (at least 70 per cent in Port Moresby) are not connected to their denomination's urban congregation (Parratt 1971: 113). Furthermore, despite the fact that local religious organizations may support or run various urban welfare projects, their origin and connections to expatriates and foreign mission bodies serves to differentiate them from the sorts of indigenously conceived and directed organizations so vital to urbanization in other parts of the world.

Formal organizations founded on other than a religious basis in urban Papua New Guinea typically lack the advantages of church groups and, except for sporting teams, have led a chequered existence. Oeser (1969) describes the fates of several such associations set up in the Hohola low-covenant housing estate in Port Moresby. The Hohola Progress Association was organized as a link between the residents and administration, and was active in a number of successful local projects (building the school, playgrounds and welfare hall) but support for it eventually declined. Oeser argues that this was due to frustration with lack of power since everything people wanted for the neighbourhood (street lighting, drainage, bus shelters, etc.) and their every major decision required administration support. The parents' and teachers' association at the primary school failed, 'perhaps because parents felt they were being directed instead of consulted' (ibid.: 57). The administration also established a women's club, run by volunteer expatriate wives of administration personnel, oriented to teaching the Hohola women to be better (by European standards) housewives and mothers. Although the budgeting and banking lessons conflicted with their traditional values concerning obligations to share rather than save wealth, and there were often problems in communication between members and European leaders, the most damaging blow dealt to the club was due to a disagreement which arose between members. A substantial sum of money was 'borrowed' from the basketball club by one of the women and opinion split along religious and ethnic lines over what action to take. The dispute spread to the Hohola Women's Club, resulting in new elections and a decline in membership. The borrower and her friends remained important members, while a number of Daru and other women dropped out, leaving a mostly Motuan and Hula membership.

The basketball teams organized by the women themselves were each made up of a core group and captain of the same ethnic background who mobilized the support of husbands and children, drawing substantial crowds to the games. 'An interesting feature was that the formal committee (president, secretary and time-keeper) was composed entirely of respected older Hohola *men*, thus repeating in miniature the social structure of the home villages' (ibid.: 63). Compared with the basketball teams, and the informal gambling groups (discussed in the fourth chapter), the multi-ethnic, expatriate-led formal associations of Hohola were largely a failure in terms of their activities, membership and meeting their own aims.

The problems confronting labour unions are another case in point (cf. Martin 1969). Although workers seem to want effective unions, creating them is another problem entirely. Potential members are, as we have seen, extremely mobile, shifting from job to job, between village and town, and have no great commitment to urban located employment despite a desire for better wages and conditions. The extreme cultural and social heterogeneity of local urbanites makes it difficult to organize around issues transcending ethnic concerns. The high rate of illiteracy and low skill levels of urban workers makes effective recruitment and participation in bureaucratic, legalistic formal organizations most unlikely, as does the small-scale and scattered nature of the nation's industrial concerns and urban work-force. The organizations themselves have been so hamstrung by colonial administrative regulations that the dynamism which would be necessary to generate active participation by workers in Papua New Guinea seems unlikely to develop. Procedural rules effectively prevent workers from calling an organized strike, and any benefits the unions are able to get in terms of wage awards, etc., are automatically extended to all workers regardless of whether or not they are union members. Finance for such necessities as full-time staff and officials has not been forthcoming (partly because the members are not aware that they periodically have to renew their membership) and this also hampers organization (Rew 1974, Stevenson 1968).

Capable organizers who possess the skill and knowledge to operate in a western-style milieu have at times been able to attract members to various organizations which seemed to have potential for promoting social change. Those which achieved the most success typically recruited members from a specific area who could readily and frequently communicate in town. Achieving some concrete aim (such as erecting a hall or buying a truck) was also an important element in maintaining the early cohesion of the organization (Metcalfe 1968: 115, Oram 1976: 139–40). But even initially promising associations, such as the Methodist and Kerema Welfare Associations in Port Moresby (the first established by local people), tend to collapse if their very narrow leadership base is eroded (Oram 1976: 136). This often occurs as a result of the promotion or transfer of a senior public servant who is president of the association. Running such a voluntary organization has also been one step along the way to a successful political career for a number of now influential government figures, whose organizations did not survive their departure (ibid.).

Those organizations which are not presently on the edge of collapse, be they regional, ethnic, work-based or political in aim and scope, recruit and operate along kinship and ethnic lines. The Lae Workers' Association and local Pangu Party branch have executive committees made up of representatives of ethnic blocs. The Lae Pangu branch can only enlist support when it convinces each ethnic unit of the need to act (Lucas 1972: 271).[1] Although powerful and dynamic groups may eventually be built upon such bases as they have in other countries, these factors have resulted in unions and other associations which are 'weak in members ... poverty stricken ... spasmodically active ... clinically if not officially

[1]   An inside account of the founding of the dominant Pangu Party in Port Moresby is contained in Prime Minister Michael Somare's autobiography (1975).

moribund' (Martin 1969: 160), and which remain marginal in terms of their effect on the overall urbanization process.

Although formal organizations are in themselves less than central to town life, some of the tasks carried out by them elsewhere are also performed in Papua New Guinea, but by informal groups organized around familiar kinship and *wantok* principles. These suffice to provide newcomers with a place to stay and an orientation to town life. The unemployed or sick seem to get supported, the dead are sent home for proper burial and small loans are raised in the absence of formal clubs or officially constituted organizations. As M. Strathern states for Hageners, 'urbanization is not expressible in terms of affiliation either to multi-ethnic or mono-ethnic voluntary organizations; it is rather to be found in ... adaptation of traditional socal forms' (1975: 364). One may legitimately wonder, however, how far these forms can go in providing for the emerging needs and aspirations of an urban population which, having established a foothold in an alien environment, will become increasingly aware that it (in addition to, or instead of, the village) is now home.

We would argue that in order to make the towns truly their own, Papua New Guineans will eventually have to develop an urban power base. As we have intimated before, their newly independent central government could greatly help by reorganizing and 'Melanesianizing' the administrative shambles inherited from Australia in such a way as to encourage public participation in urban decision-making. If the government is willing to do this, and the people themselves can organize more effective formal ethnic and work-based associations, the remaining hollowness and colonial atmosphere of the nation's towns will in time disappear. But for the present it is clear that (as pointed out before) government rules and regulations are inhibiting rather than promoting the processes of adaptation of towns and townsmen. A concrete example of this can be seen in the dearth of indigenous urban business activity. The colour and bustle (and, of course, the income) generated by local entrepreneurial activity in other Third World towns is almost completely absent in Papua New Guinea, except perhaps on market days. The following examination of some of the difficulties encountered by Papua New Guinea's indigenous businessmen, particularly in their dealings with government departments (Andrews 1975, Fitzpatrick and Blaxter 1976), will serve to illustrate in greater depth the sort of institutional problems we have been discussing.

Urban businessmen

Relatively few urban Papua New Guineans are self-employed. The overwhelming majority of those individuals who work for themselves are involved in one-person operations in the 'informal sector'. A few women may sew clothing at home or sell produce from their gardens, while men fish from their own canoes or take a lawnmower from door to door. In every town individuals sell small carvings or sea shells: in Port Moresby they often sit on the sidewalks of the main shopping areas with their wares on a mat or a piece of cloth beside them, while in Mount Hagen and Goroka people walk along the streets with a carved mask or bamboo jew's harp in their hands offering it to any European they pass. Individuals or small groups of Papua New Guineans may also run trade stores in urban and peri-urban villages, or own trucks (which confer a great deal of prestige) and canoes, which are typically used to run passengers into town. Some men will even hire a few *wantok* to help them in the course of casual sub-contracting jobs, but their work is usually irregular and on a very limited scale (Andrews 1975, Oram 1967). By-and-large, these forms of self-employment are simply seen as a source of ready cash, or a means of maintaining oneself in the town – an extension, so to speak, of the rural subsistence garden.

A very small number of Papua New Guineans, however, have become businessmen in the western sense of the word, developing truly non-traditional forms of business organization and competing in fields which previously were exploited only by expatriates. In a study of the indigenous businessmen in Port Moresby (nearly all of whom are Papuans from urban villages or areas with a long history of contact), Andrews (1975) found a variety of types reflecting the diverse contexts within which they operate.

The older established businessmen (all of whom are members of the Motu and Koita groups native to the Port Moresby area) entered the field at a time when the administration was making no effort to encourage indigenous urban enterprises and few people believed that Papua New Guineans were capable of making a go of it in what was an entirely expatriate business arena. That these men were able to develop successful businesses in such an environment was a remarkable accomplishment and depended largely on their managerial talents, assertiveness and the early support of their home villages. Basing themselves in their own urban or peri-urban village community, they could count on local labour, a certain amount of capital and, most of all, the villagers' patronage of their business (typically passenger transport or retailing). But once established, these businessmen could diversify their activities, expanding beyond the limited local market for their services and also getting outside finance through hire-purchase agreements with finance companies. At the same time, however, they continued to live in their home villages, in the same material circumstances as their co-villagers.

In order to understand these men and the problems they have in dealing with government agencies, it is essential to realize that status in their community and traditional exchange relationships remain very important to them and their activities. Far from abandoning these ties when they entered into the business domain, older established indigenous businessmen used their varied resources and comparative affluence to build up, manipulate and expand them beyond their traditional scope. They also do a great deal in the way of contributing to and participating in church and village welfare work. In this way businessmen gain prestige and sometimes support for positions of leadership in the village or wider contexts (much in the style of the traditional big-man). At the same time there is an ideology of equality so that jealousy and the threat of sorcery or physical violence tends to be taken seriously. It is important for these businessmen to strike some sort of balance in defining their roles in their communities and in their businesses. This point is dramatically illustrated by the case of the oldest indigenous business in Port Moresby, Mirikuro Transport, owned by two brothers who left the public service in 1960 to go into business for themselves with one second-hand truck. The company had developed steadily for seven years, running a whole fleet of trucks with forty workers, when the elder brother was murdered. Although the case was never solved, envy of the ambitious man's success is widely thought to have been the motive for the crime. The younger brother, Walo, is convinced that his ill-health is caused by sorcery and has paid a number of known sorcerers for protection, but this has not helped. When his new partner and assistant manager wanted to replace some vehicles that were in poor condition, Walo decided against this because of the jealousy that would be aroused by so conspicuous a display of affluence as the purchase of new trucks. For the same reason he refused to allow his junior wife to redecorate and furnish their house in European style.

One of the problems the older businessmen faced was the very alien nature of the business culture they had to deal with. Working within the model of the small business, and particularly at a time when the administration was not willing to make concessions to indigenous businessmen, they felt at a distinct disadvantage in making bids for tenders, or when competing with European businessmen in general. The bureaucracy was strange and difficult to deal with, all the senior officers of the relevant government departments were expatriates, there were no Papua New Guineans on the Supply and Tender Board, few local businessmen tended to mix socially with expatriates and thus were not privy to the sorts of inside information they might have found useful, and at least one of Andrews' informants believed that the tenders were rigged. These older Papua New Guineans tend to run their businesses in a rather individualistic way in that, even though they may have frequent contacts with each other in formal, informal, social and business contexts, they have not made use of this network to unite as a pressure group to deal with the government departments and private companies whose policies affect them in many ways. Instead, they try to cope with their problems on an individual and competitive basis (again, in the style of big-men) and are consequently less effective (Andrews 1975).

For the younger men who have entered business more recently, the situation has been rather different on a number of counts. To begin with, they are better educated than the older men, generally having some secondary education as opposed to only a few years of primary school. Furthermore, these younger men have typically gone into business at the instigation of an expatriate sponsor or government agency devoted to developing indigenous enterprises. (By-and-large, business is not so attractive to young, educated Papua New Guineans, who are in great demand by the public service and private industry, as are formally trained tradesmen.) While older businessmen were sometimes able to get contracts from former employers, the younger men were typically taken into partnership or promoted into a business by a former employer and loaned the money to buy into it by the Development Bank. Their businesses are not tied to their villages as were those of the older men. Indeed, some provide services which cater largely for the expatriate community such as a milk round and a commercial cleaning establishment. Others have gone into manufacturing. While all have been loaned money or provided services by the Development Bank, they have tended to avoid its control as much as possible. Young businessmen deal directly with the business community and apparently are not as much put off by the fact that it is dominated by expatriates (possibly because of their experiences with their own sponsors with whom they are said to identify). These men tend to have fewer personal ties with their employees and adopt a more strictly 'boss'-like stance in relationship to them, although there is much variation in their policies concerning the hiring of *wantoks*. They also differ in the kind of role they play in their home communities, generally having greater freedom in this respect than the older and more established men, who bring many ongoing traditionally-based relationships into business with them. The younger men are more likely to take up the sorts of activities that western businessmen tend to be involved in such as the Lions Club, the Chamber of Commerce, political parties, etc. (ibid.: 114–32).

Both types of businessmen are anxious to expand their concerns. The older men, however, are more likely to diversify their interests while the younger tend to reinvest and build up their original enterprise. There seems to be a positive value placed on having one's fingers in a number of pies, but there are a few reasons why this may have an especial appeal for the older businessmen. First of all, being involved in a variety of business activities gives them access to a greater range of resources to manipulate in carrying on village and wider exchange relationships. Diversification allows them to expand without doing anything on a conspicuously large scale. This is good because they take jealousy and attacks through sorcery very seriously: some of them go so far as to pay protection money to local people known to be adept at witchcraft and employ sorcerers from outside groups who have a reputation for having especially powerful magic. Furthermore, diversification provides a certain amount of security or insurance for these men who have probably come to expect from long experience that their success in any particular area is likely to be limited by factors beyond their control such as market size, government policy or the decisions of large private firms (e.g. whether the firm will use the fork-lift services owned by Papua New Guineans or organize their own). Only recently has the government begun restricting tenders (typically for smaller-scale jobs) in order to encourage indigenous enterprise (ibid.: 64–5, 104).

As late as 1968, a development programme prepared by the government emphasized rural, agricultural-based activities, and while brief reference was made to the fact that indigenes would be helped to establish cottage industries and businesses in retailing and such services as plumbing and contracting by the Development Bank and other agencies, no guidelines were set for the implementation of these policies. The Development Bank began lending in the late 1960s and much of the money borrowed by Papua New Guineans was for rural activities and averaged between $1000 and $2000. More than half the money went to expatriates in much larger loans and also to a handful of joint enterprises. While this was probably a substantial improvement over the previous situation, Crocombe (1969) has described the plans for promoting Papua New Guinean participation in the economy as 'tokenism'. He argues that they are aimed more towards supporting the big expatriate businesses by providing them with cheap labour, investors and 'peasant producers for expatriate commerce to buy produce from and supply goods to', while giving the people little substantive representation on statutory bodies and only enough training 'to result in long term dependence on expatriates' (Andrews 1975: 11–20).

Certainly it is true that until 1970 the Department of Business Development advisory services were mostly involved in helping trade store owners in the urban villages with stock-taking, and filing tax forms for them and for the owners of passenger transport vehicles. The Development Bank was mostly dealing with small, rural projects. It was only later when the Department of Business Development opened its Business Promotions Centres and the Development Bank started its

Projects Department that they began to promote indigenous business concerns in the towns.

The Business Promotions Centre in Port Moresby provides advice and help with paper-work for indigenous businessmen as well as renting out cheap workshop space for fledgling enterprises. Their tenants, according to Andrews, have had very limited success. By-and-large, they have been auto mechanics, panel beaters, etc., with little or no formal education and training, for whom a fling at 'business' involved no risk. The staff of the Business Promotions Centre (called Business Advisory Officers) provided them with free book-keeping, banking and managerial services, but did not have the technical skills to help with making quotes or quality control. Some of the businesses collapsed because of a falling-out between the partners and also because they did not get enough work. The Business Promotions Centre workshops were not on the main roads and the common lack of confidence in Papua New Guineans meant that they were frequently approached when the customer did not have the cash on hand to go to one of the expatriate-owned garages. The workshops also tended to become social centres with *wantok* hanging around, sometimes doing odd jobs for pay and sometimes borrowing equipment and work-space to fix their own cars. It is interesting that the two tenants who were evicted (for being behind in rent, dishonest or just 'difficult') set up for themselves independently in other parts of the town, saying that they much preferred working on their own with no 'official interference' (ibid.: 133–57).

Certainly there are problems in communications on several levels of the Business Promotions Centre's operation. The field staff (Business Advisory Officers) complain about being snowed under with paper-work and writing reports for headquarters, which headquarters staff insists is necessary for effective planning. Implementation, on the other hand, is held to be entirely the field staff's affair and they get no guidelines about it from headquarters, just as the field staff have no part in the planning process. 'As a result of this lack of direction, staff have dealt with proposals mainly on an ad hoc basis. The work of the centre has not been actively promoted and ... the range of activities has so far been fairly limited' (ibid.: 154). In the area of economic development in general, many goals have been set, but few strategies laid out.

There are also difficulties in co-ordinating the activities of different government departments. For example, the Department of Trade and Industry are concerned with attracting foreign investment. At one point they were anxious to secure for a foreign company the special privileges given by the government to the entrepreneur who pioneers a new industry (in this case, the manufacture of footwear) in Papua New Guinea. They were virtually in competition with the agencies developing indigenous business which were applying for the same pioneer certificate on behalf of a Papua New Guinean-owned manufacturing enterprise (which finally did get it) (ibid.: 167–8).

Misunderstandings between field staff and clients are not uncommon. For example, a trade store owner who is barely literate in English finds the Business Advisory Officer's communications (written or spoken) incomprehensible, while a businessman takes offence at a remark which is meant as a friendly joke, or perhaps does not feel up to arguing with the field officer so simply agrees with his directives but proceeds to ignore them in practice. Perhaps most frustrating to all involved are those situations where the staff and clients have entirely different goals. A classic case of this is the Buang Taxi Trucks, a fleet of passenger transport vehicles which operate within Port Moresby and are owned by migrants from an area near Lae. The company is run by a five-member committee which includes a hired clerk/Secretary, a Business Advisory Officer and three prominent Buang men. The Business Advisory Officer has worked with them for years to try to make the business a more profitable one, but the Buang leaders typically act against his advice so as not to look weak before the rest of the Buang group. Furthermore, the migrants see their trucks as a source of ready cash and are not concerned with the ins and outs of profits and depreciation. They tend to send the money to their home villages with an eye towards starting prestigious businesses there such as pig, poultry or cattle raising, which some have already accomplished. They prefer to buy new trucks by raising more share contributions from the town-dwelling Buang migrants. The Business Advisory Officer feels that it should be a profitable enterprise even though some of the operations run at a loss. He is constantly pressed by headquarters for profit figures, and when he presses the Buang in turn, he reaps only resentment for what is regarded as his high-handed interference (ibid.: 147–9).

Andrews finds that there are three trends in the relationships between field staff and clients: at one extreme is the utter dependence on the Business Advisory Officer by the ones who have no hope of making it in business, at the other end is resentment which results in the client leaving, and there is a middle ground of 'ill-feeling tempered by an awareness of the benefits conferred by or expected from an association with BPC and by the businessmen's lack of self-confidence' (ibid.: 157).

The Projects Department of the Development Bank was set up rather differently (it is semi-autonomous from the rest of the agency) and has a somewhat more dynamic approach to developing urban indigenous business than the Business Promotions Centres. They often arrange the transfer of businesses from expatriates to indigenous hands (commonly where an expatriate sponsor wishes to promote his protégé into the business or take him in as a partner); but they also scout out good business ventures independently and then look for a likely Papua New Guinean to train to run the enterprise and gradually buy into it. The Development Bank Officers in the Projects Department have a great deal of freedom and fewer communications problems than the Business Advisory Officers, both internally and with clients. But enthusiastic as they are, they are not really trained to teach management skills, and while many of their clients are willing to leave the book-keeping and important decision-making in the hands of Development Bank officers, some want to manage on their own and this occasionally leads to conflict (ibid.: 158–75).

Sometimes the bureaucratic controls put on the indigenous businessman as prerequisites for financial and other assistance are counter-productive for the enterprise. Contractors in Port Moresby are typically held up by the Development Bank's procedure of not granting loans until a particular tender has been won. The contractor loses precious time as the completion deadline is written into the contract and they must wait until the Development Bank processes their loan and frees the necessary funds before they can get started. Sometimes the contractors have to work under a system where all their purchases must be signed and approved by the Business Advisory Officer before they can be paid for, and this means they have to waste time running back and forth between the suppliers and the Business Promotions Centre offices. Since this system does not allow them to keep extra supplies on hand, even more trips have to be made (ibid.:199–200).

Some contractors (and other indigenous businessmen) can minimize these controls. Although they are dependent to varying degrees on the loans, support, advice and help of these agencies, the businessmen provide the staff with a *raison d'être* and when they succeed it reflects well on the field officers involved with them. Thus a Business Advisory Officer will (understandably) get more satisfaction from working with the more successful Papua New Guineans (who are generally less dependent on him anyway), and he tends to be willing to bend the rules a little bit for them (ibid.: 201–2).

There is a limit to how much bending the rules allow, however. A number of critics have pointed out how the regulations affecting business in Papua New Guinea have restricted the growth of indigenous enterprise. Laws governing the setting up of companies, building standards, relations with employees, etc. are all based on an Australian model. They are frustrating for the indigenous businessman for a number of reasons. He is unfamiliar with the legalisms and this forces him to depend on the help of expatriate advisors for many details. The standards are unrealistically high and necessitate enormous (for Papua New Guineans) capital outlay. Because of this, the local businessman is often dependent upon the Development Bank for loans and this in turn involves him in more unfamiliar red tape and the irritating controls we discussed above. Although Andrews found that a couple of businessmen had got loans from family, in no case were they able to rely on kin groups for financing on any large scale. This contrasts with the situation in rural Papua New Guinea and much of urban Africa (Nigeria, for example) where most businessmen were set up in business with money from parents and relatives (ibid.: 69).

Numerous laws have been enacted for the purpose of limiting competition in favour of large-scale, typically expatriate-owned enterprises. Many more laws that are much in line with Australian health codes, suitable perhaps for a modern industrial economy, but irrelevant to Papua New Guinean towns, have also had the practical effect of limiting or making impossible many areas which indigenous entrepreneurs might otherwise exploit. For example, the law which prescribes that a ten-gallon water-tank and pump be attached to any mobile prepared-food pedlar's vehicle effectively precludes businesses operating from cycles. Consequently, Papua New Guinea does not have the 'bazaar economy', the hordes of street vendors and small shops and stalls with a wide range of activities that flourish in the towns of most other Third World nations (Fitzpatrick and Blaxter 1976).

It seems fair to say that business in urban Papua New Guinea requires not the adaptation of traditional forms so much as the adoption of non-traditional ones, although it certainly should not preclude the retention of traditional social styles.

To begin with, as we have described above, the legal and economic framework which is part of Papua New Guinea's colonial heritage in no way encourages (and, in a number of ways, discourages) small-scale indigenous urban enterprise and the informal sector in general. The whole expatriate-dominated business community and western styles of business organization are alien to Papua New Guineans – even those who have had a relatively great deal of contact with Europeans. Yet in order to be substantially successful, the indigenous businessman has to adapt himself to these western forms.

This may cause difficulties in dealing with *wantok*. For example, the owners of three of the concerns studied by Andrews (all of them factories) say that they never hire *wantok* because they tend to take advantage of their special relationship with the 'boss'. But this stance is a rare one. Most indigenous businessmen with a regular staff do employ *wantok*. Some feel obliged to provide employment; some seek to avoid feelings of jealousy. Some businessmen say they prefer to employ *wantok* because they can communicate better with them and trust them. It is true that *wantok* tend to be in positions of responsibility and better paid than the other employees, but this may be because the unskilled labourers tend to be Highlanders while the businessmen are all from areas with a long history of contact so that their *wantok* generally have had some formal education (ibid.: 61–2). Relations with *wantok* also depend on how close the businessman's home area is to the city. A contractor from Hula (a village about 100 km from Port Moresby), for example, would be better off in this regard than one from Porebada which is much closer in. *Wantok* from Hula are much less dependent on cash wages and so are easier to pull in and out of employment with the fluctuating demand for labour, whereas a Porebadan businessman might be under greater pressure to maintain high levels of employment of village tradesmen. Some businessmen tend to hire younger *wantok* while others employ members of their own peer group. In the latter situation many ongoing relationships and obligations may also become involved and this can result in concessions being made to the *wantok* in the course of the job and can complicate the boss's role relationships considerably (ibid.: 200–1).

Secondly, the complexities of handling a business in terms of accounting, filing tax forms and preparing quotes and bids for tenders are outside the experience of many Papua New Guineans. Often they depend on government agencies to perform these tasks for them.

The high level of capital expenditure presently necessary to start a business forces the indigenous businessman to seek loans from government agencies making him even more dependent on a bureaucracy that he usually finds strange and difficult to manipulate effectively. In the course of protecting the government's investments, the agencies may place a number of controls on the businessman, to the point where he may feel he is entirely at the mercy of government officials and development agency fieldworkers.

The field officers tend to push the businessmen to expand, sometimes to the point where they are no longer able or willing to handle the management duties involved. The officers may take over more and more of the responsibilities of dealing with the wider business community (suppliers, customers, etc.) and the major decision-making for the concern as well; occasionally they exceed not only their mandate as field officers, but their talents and capabilities as well (ibid.: 73–4).

Many indigenous businessmen are forced to submit to this erosion of their autonomy and independence but it generally does not sit well with their own conceptions of what business is about and the roles they wish to play. Although the younger men are (to varying degrees) more likely to look to business as a way to achieving a new sort of life-style, most indigenous businessmen are concerned with their status in their home communities, and the prestige that they get from success in their enterprises is comparable in many ways, as we have intimated before, to that of the traditional big-man. Their affluence and the diversity of their interests allows them to attract followers and they are in a position to manipulate a variety of goods, services and people. But most importantly, they feel that their businesses and the money they produce should make them independent and able to support village and church activities. It is this that can make them important people – not wealth in and of itself, but how they use it to benefit the community (ibid.: 70–1).

The major difficulties in developing indigenous urban business are the problems that Papua New Guineans have in dealing with an alien bureaucracy that seems set on destroying their autonomy. The bureaucracy and the bureaucrats themselves show little understanding or acceptance of the desires of indigenous businessmen for prestige and independence, rather than just profits.

In this chapter we have maintained that the effective 'Papua New Guineanization' of the towns has reached something of a plateau. The ongoing creative processes of adaptation emphasized in earlier chapters have yet to be successfully manipulated in such a way that local people can extend their (increasingly pervasive) socio-cultural idioms into formal urban institutions. We have seen that this is due both to the disorganization of their inherited bureaucracy and to the present ineffective state of indigenous voluntary organizations. Concrete examples of the experiences of businessmen (among Papua New Guinea's most successful participants in western-oriented activities) have highlighted some specifics of the problematic nature of interaction between urbanites and government departments. It is at this stage too early to tell whether or not, or in what way, urbanites and governmental institutions will reach an accommodation that will allow for the further development of the forces which are creating Papua New Guinean towns out of colonial places.

7. Comparisons and conclusions

In the introduction to this monograph it was stated that ruralness plays an important part in urban life in Papua New Guinea, where the social process of urbanization involves the adaptation, modification, retention and abandonment of rurally derived behavioural idioms and styles in response to various aspects of urban society. We further maintained that the most interesting social action going on in the towns is contained in the synthesis of new social systems arising from the interaction between a colonially based social order and a mélange of tribal people, which formerly defined mutually exclusive social worlds. Now that the data and main themes contained in the literature concerned with Papua New Guinea's towns have been discussed, it is appropriate to summarize and reflect upon the general nature of this ongoing synthesis. We should, however, bear in mind that the subtle interrelationship between rural and urban behaviour in urban Papua New Guinea has been differently interpreted by the authors whose research has provided the foundation for this monograph. As perhaps not everyone would agree with the perspective taken here, it will be useful to counterpose briefly various views of the urbanization process (some were mentioned in passing above) and relate them to our own approach and conclusions.

Views of urbanization

Although everyone seems to agree that positing a rural–urban opposition which contrasts city ways with village ways is not a useful perspective for Papua New Guinea, some anthropologists go so far as to reverse the stance taken by certain urban sociologists who maintain that urbanization results in the disintegration of rural types of social institutions. These anthropologists suggest that urbanization has either not occurred in Papua New Guinea's towns or that their informants' behaviour is so permeated by village attitudes and concerns that its significance can only be understood as a rural strategy.

The strongest exponents of the rural approach are the Salisburys (1970, 1972) and Zimmerman (1973). The latter maintains that the Buang of Lae and Port Moresby are not urbanized at all because they neither participate in urban institutions (such as schools and voluntary associations) nor contribute to the urban setting. As was mentioned in the

130

section of Chapter Four dealing with life in the settlements, she feels that it is foolish to talk about urbanization when so many aspects of their life-style are transported directly from the village to the towns. The Salisburys' conception of Sianes as conducting a rural strategy pays most attention to their village commitments and future plans to return home with capital or skills for rural enterprises. Their sojourn in town is merely a means to that end and involves no fundamental socio-cultural change that would encourage us to call the Siane urbanized.

One might perhaps accept these characteristics at face value (explaining such behaviour as the result of the recent migration of unskilled, uncertain groups of people who have little impact on the urban social system) were it not for the contrary interpretations of other authors. Oeser (1969), for example, found that rurally oriented relationships, far from precluding successful adaptation to urban life, might well facilitate it. Although her findings would encourage us to agree that complete ethnic encapsulation (such as that reported for the Buang) is limiting, the women who coped best with life in Hohola housing estate in Port Moresby were those who maintained both rurally based and urban ties. Siane and Buang solidarity, often expressed in terms of common rural plans and aspirations, would not isolate them from the town's influence if they developed relationships with other people. The seeming marginality and sparseness of such relationships may in fact be more explainable in terms of their position in the urban system (cf. our discussion of interaction patterns in Chapter Five) than the rural ties *per se*. In other words, the 'rural strategy' is at least partially an epiphenomenon of urban experiences and is therefore an aspect of urbanization itself.

We have also seen that Ryan (1968, 1970) stresses continuity and interrelatedness between the Toaripi people living in Port Moresby and those back home in Uritai village. She feels, however, that the Toaripi are townsmen and resolves the rural–urban dilemma by conceptualizing Toaripi society itself as a bi-local (rural–urban) social system. Since rural and urban events, relationships and styles are so interrelated for the Toaripi, she feels that an analysis of the Toaripi as urbanites or participants in a purely urban system in Port Moresby would be incomplete. Although this view may be defendable from a Toaripi standpoint, it does evade major questions that are relevant to an understanding of the towns themselves. Whatever role rural events have in urban life, it is important to recognize that the towns are social fields in themselves which deserve analysis. This, of course, necessitates a shift in perspective from a discussion of the life-styles of a particular ethnographically defined group of people to a consideration of the dynamic relationship between life-styles and the urban environment. But despite their potential problems in this regard, mono-ethnic urban studies can still shed light upon the general nature of the urban system. If an anthropologist is aware of the limitations of such an approach and is willing to maintain an appreciation of the wider context of 'rurally oriented' behaviour, an idea of its implications for the urban system may emerge.

In her study of Hageners in Port Moresby, M. Strathern clearly states that her main concern is with that small group of urbanites rather than the town itself. She does, however, discuss 'urban Hagen society' and the differences and similarities between it and rural Hagen society (1975: 363–420).

From a Hagen point of view, the town is an alternative rather than part of a bi-local social system, one that allows for an escape from or post-ponement of rural adult responsibilities as well as the chance to experience new things. When Hageners live in Port Moresby they do not exchange their previous forms of behaviour for urban ones, rather 'Hagenness is an essential part of urbanness' (ibid.: 400). The talk of returning home, of rural business opportunities, etc., which so convinces others that New Guineans are conducting rural strategies, are seen as essential components of the creation of an urban Hagen social life. Such talk of home and the relating of urban activities to village concerns are symbolic statements essential to the growth of an urban community. They provide a potent expression of mutuality and are a force in themselves in keeping people interacting, aiding their mutual adjustment to urban life. The establishment of urban sub-cultures is a crucial function of 'rural strategies' in Papua New Guinea's towns. To overlook this and con-centrate on the dubious future such statements imply (that people will go home and become businessmen) involves a serious omission on the part of the researcher.

The tendency to perceive urban life-styles in terms of rural values and equivalents has further implications. M. Strathern (ibid.: 418) says that urban Hageners do not view even distinctive aspects of their way of life as contrasting with that of the village. Rural–urban difference in behaviour is evaluated in terms of the standing which equivalent actions at home would bring people. Their lack of responsibilities, businesses, and wives, and their freedom to promenade around in town, for example, are seen as comparable to traditional pre-adult life-style and activities. Urbanites often stress their unimportance in such terms and so are reticent and reluctant to act in the way important men at home do, thus leaving urban Hagen society relatively leaderless. Although other groups may not have this particular problem, Strathern's point, that such interpretations of urban behaviour inhibit the growth of an ideology which could provide a counter to rurally phrased ones, is probably generally true. The view taken throughout this monograph, that a 'rural orientation' is a type of urban ideology which has important implications for the urbanization process, directs our attention towards the dynamics of that process itself, and away from a facile rejection of such an ideology's significance.

One may, however, question the sorts of implications this has for the urban system as a whole. Rew characterizes Port Moresby as being made up of three autonomous urban role systems defined by kinship, race and work relationships (1974: 213–30). Individuals select and act upon norms and values appropriate to the role situation they happen to be in, e.g. generalized reciprocity in interactions with kinsmen, deference towards expatriates and task-oriented behaviour while on the job. The recasting of rural social referents as general principles of association in the town is seen as the social cement which mediates between these otherwise separate role systems, giving a measure of solidarity to an otherwise segmented social system. The drawing of residents into new associations is, of course, an essential dynamic of the urbanization process. But, as we have seen above, strong segmental tendencies remain important ingredients of the social life of Papua New Guinea's towns and these also find expression in rurally derived social idioms.

If cities are meeting places for diverse cultures, levelling devices which integrate disparate peoples into new super-regional wholes, and nuclei for the 'formation of national tradition' (Simic 1973: 11), Papua New Guinea's towns have barely begun to fill such a role. Nevertheless, we believe that the dialectical interaction between the country's people and its towns is beginning to produce a unique and distinctly national (as opposed to colonial) type of urban centre.

Papua New Guinea urbanization in wider perspective: points of comparison

Although Papua New Guineans are developing their own urban social systems it is important to realize that they are participating in a type of social process that has involved much of the rest of the world's people for a considerably longer period of time. The urbanization of the Third World is universally recognized as one of the fundamental social transformations of our time and it is, of course, pertinent to ask where Papua New Guinea fits into the overall range of present experience. We do not feel, however, that it would suffice to answer this question by making simple comparisons of statistics on the urban population trends, economic development, spatial patterns, etc., of different nations. Because we have been discussing urbanization as a social process, we must instead consider the sorts of factors and processes which are most fundamentally involved in the production of new kinds of social systems in urban locations.

The variety of urban experience in newly developing countries is so great, however, that one author of a frequently cited comparative volume has seemingly despaired of developing a useful typology of towns in the Third World (Breese 1966: 50). Although we agree that typologies may be criticized, especially for being overly general, our purpose in this section is merely to provide some points of difference and similarity between towns in Papua New Guinea and elsewhere as a device to help the reader more fully appreciate what we feel are the relatively unique aspects of the local situation.

One fruitful way of approaching the problem of enormous urban diversity is suggested by McGee (1971), who has noted that there are three general types of town, the pre-industrial, colonial, and industrial. The most industrial towns are of course found in the West and Japan which was the only nation to industrialize successfully while maintaining independence from the western powers (Southall 1973a: 8). Products of the industrial revolution, these metropolises house a generally stable urban work-force characterized by a great variety of skills and experience that has few if any ties to the land. Pre-industrial towns were indigenously developed, very often by a feudal type of society, and served mainly as slowly growing religious, administrative and trading centres. Colonial towns, on the other hand, are rarely fully industrial or indigenous but have been developed by foreign powers in the course of imperialistic expansion and reflect the needs and plans of outsiders. These cities frequently developed into centres of substantial (and initially often circular) urban migration as well as becoming the capitals of new nations.

Interacting with the urban types so briefly delineated above we may also distinguish very broad societal types. Modern industrial cities are associated with developed western-style societies, as pre-industrial towns (such as Mecca, Saudi Arabia) are with peasantries or societies which retain certain feudal traits. Colonial towns have been established in both peasant and tribal areas, such as India and Papua New Guinea. These have even occasionally been grafted on to existing pre-industrial centres (e.g. in India and West Africa). A considerable mixture of societal and urban types may occur, however, as when westerners and former peasants come to fill certain new niches in colonial cities in pre-industrial and tribal areas, or when peasants and tribal people migrate to western metropolises. This picture is further complicated by variation in a constellation of important 'external' factors (Mitchell 1966) which we will discuss below. The situation of greatest relevance to our comparative discussion is certainly the colonial city set in the midst of a tribal population.

A more detailed model of the colonial city has been developed by Bellam (1970) whose research was in Honiara, capital of the former

British Solomon Islands Protectorate, which borders on Papua New Guinea. He notes that colonial towns are characterized by the following: external origin, orientation and dependence; dual economies dominated by non-indigenes; polarity between natives and expatriates; a high proportion of unskilled and semi-skilled workers; an ambivalence towards urban places on the part of the indigenous people; the emergence of an indigenous bureaucratic urban élite; and a 'parasitic' relationship between the town and its hinterland. Although, as Bellam notes, the model neither explains the way urbanites perceive the situation nor the effects of the town's growth on indigenous institutions and behaviour, we are clearly dealing with a set of overarching factors which greatly influence urbanization as a social process.

A more general set of factors acting on all towns, which we can combine with our model of the colonial city to help explain variation, has been posited by Mitchell. He calls these 'external' factors because they (like the elements of Bellam's model) produce a social matrix within which urban behaviour itself (the real subject of sociological analysis) takes place. The factors are: population density, which enables a wide range of contacts in towns; mobility, or the degree and pattern of migration and movement within towns; heterogeneity; demographic structure; level and type of economic differentiation and social stratification; and administrative and political limitations on citizens.

A truly in-depth comparative study of urbanization would have the extraordinarily complicated task of discussing the many combinations and various expressions of these characteristics as they exist throughout the world. One would probably find in the end that each town was in many ways unique. We can, however, note certain broad similarities and differences in a range of factors which help in our task of discussing Papua New Guinean towns in comparative perspective.

Papua New Guinea, Latin America, South-East Asia and Africa

Bellam suggests that Africa, South-East Asia and the Pacific are three areas where the colonial city is common. Latin America is presumably excluded because although most of its cities resulted from Spanish settlement, medieval Iberian colonialism differed in many ways from later post-industrial expansion. Latin American towns do indeed seem in many ways unlike their Papua New Guinean counterparts. In addition to the greater size, antiquity, and originally Iberian colonial framework of Latin American cities, we may note that rural Latin Americans are much more affected by national and world economic and political forces than are rural Papua New Guineans. They come to non-indigenous cities apparently seeking to integrate into the wider society which has largely broken down their pre-contact tribal social systems and created a dependent peasantry. Highland Peruvians of Quecha Indian background are for example said to be undergoing a process of evolving into Spanish-speaking Peruvians in Lima (Doughty 1970). They migrate to towns characterized by an established and pervasive class hierarchy which contrasts with the more ethnically stratified rural areas. Latin Americans are much more likely to organize formally in the face of urban adversity than Papua New Guineans: they have, for example, undertaken carefully planned and executed invasions of vacant land for housing. Poverty in the countryside also seems to close off any viable village option from many Latin American urbanites, and a tendency to drop rural traits and identify with the city has been noted, especially for those who make out well in town (Southall 1973a: 12). Since Papua New Guinean cities are possessed of traits almost opposite to those just mentioned perhaps we should look to the other areas suggested for closer comparability.

South-East Asia also presents features which are likely to make urbanization as a social process there different in a number of important ways from the Papua New Guinean situation. In terms of our general typology most urbanites there are peasants, not tribesmen, and some cities are indigenous to the states in the region. There are, of course, a considerable number of ex-colonial cities in South-East Asia, but these seem more dominated by foreign populations than are those in Papua New Guinea. Kuala Lumpur, Malaysia, for example, grew from a Chinese mining centre into a capital city still containing a majority Chinese population. Malay peasants migrating into the city are faced with a situation in which the pre-eminent groups living in the town are non-indigenous (McGee 1971: 147). Although Papua New Guinean towns were also recently dominated by expatriates, the smallness of the Chinese population and the post-independence political impotence of Europeans means that the country and its towns are less likely to remain divided into political and economic spheres differentially controlled by indigenous and non-native groups as was the case in the classic South-East Asian plural society. In common with Latin America, many South-East Asians also seem to be 'pushed' out of the countryside because of rural population pressure and poverty into towns that may well be crowded enough to make their nations 'over-urbanized' and act as a constraint to further economic development.

When we look to Africa and the Pacific Islands other than Papua New Guinea we are of course moving the discussions towards areas which are apt to be most similar to our own case study.

A number of authors with Pacific Island experience have mentioned that urbanization in sub-Saharan Africa shares a number of features with the South Pacific (Bedford 1973, Bellam 1970, Levine 1977, Rew 1974). That this should be the case seems fairly obvious when one considers that black Africa contains many tribal societies and colonial cities. It is also a place where urbanization is recent and of small scale demographically compared to the rest of the world. For example, only about 11 per cent of Africans live in towns of over 20,000 people (Gutkind 1974: 310). Papua New Guinea's urban population of 9 per cent is fairly close to this, although the enumerated urban areas include much smaller centres. Africa, then, may well be the area (outside the Pacific Islands) most similar to Papua New Guinea, since the rural background, colonial experiences, timing, degree and recency of urbanization are all at least generally comparable.

Some caution is, however, necessary. Pre-industrial urbanism was common, especially in West Africa, where great states and trading kingdoms such as Ghana, Benin, Songhai, Oyo, Ashanti and Dahomey existed prior to European colonial penetration. Some towns (such as Kano and Ibadan, Nigeria) present a mixture of pre-industrial and colonial styles of urbanism. In addition, certain areas of Africa are considerably more industrial. Urbanization of the Copperbelt (Zambia) and other parts of southern Africa brought Africans to mines and compounds where they faced a different set of problems than most Papua New Guineans or West Africans. One early Copperbelt study, for example, charts the development of a union movement which transcended tribalism in Luanshya (Epstein 1958). The harsh restrictions placed upon blacks in present-day South Africa, and their fundamental opposition to whites, reminds one that urbanization in Africa has divergent forms, especially between those areas which were settler colonies and those which were not.

Perhaps it is really East Africa which has the closest non-Pacific parallels with Melanesia's experience of urbanization (Bellam 1970: 95). Like Melanesia, that part of the continent (excluding Ethiopia) had almost no pre-colonial urban tradition. Its people were more generally tribal than peasant and their colonial experience was similarly Anglo-Saxon. The cities of East Africa were also less dominated by Europeans than those of southern Africa. There does, however, seem to be greater tension between East Africans and Asians over the issue of economic domination (e.g. Uganda's former Indians) than is found in urban Papua New Guinea.

With such strong similarities (and despite its array of differences) the general African urban situation may, because of its somewhat more developed form, give us clues to possible future trends in Papua New Guinea. Ethnicity, for example, seems a dominant theme in the social systems of towns in both areas, but as noted earlier, Africans form strong urban ethnic organizations while Papua New Guineans do not. The maintenance of kin ties and rural land rights by urban Africans, their pattern of visiting, plans to retire to the village, and their playing down of the significance of class divisions in certain situations (Ferraro 1973, Grillo 1974, Lloyd 1974), are also familiar themes. But in Africa a tendency towards increasing residence in towns (and less circular rural–urban migration) has been noted, especially in areas where people have been allowed freedom of choice (Bedford 1973). Going 'home', a very strongly expressed intention in Nigeria, nevertheless remains a dream unfulfilled according to Plotnicov (1970). We might expect that as time goes on urban Papua New Guineans will, like their African counterparts, become more positive and less 'ambivalent' townsmen. As a generation comes of age in the towns, they may (despite continuing ideological ties to rural areas) come to identify more strongly with urban life-styles, form stronger urban-oriented formal organizations, and develop a more 'stable' pattern of continuous urban residence.

Papua New Guinean towns and the Island South Pacific

Despite important similarities with Africa, it should come as no surprise that Papua New Guinean towns are really most like those of their nearby Pacific Island neighbours. But even here, in such a closely defined area, we find a great range of urban experiences, one which mirrors in microcosm the variety of patterns of urbanization and points out the difficulties of making any but very general comparisons between different regions.

A number of South Pacific islands have developed from settler colonies into states or territories which contain essentially Euro-American towns. Hawaiians, for instance, have the 'dubious honor of being perhaps the first urbanized and proletarianized Pacific Island population'. Most now work in urban areas such as Honolulu, and have little memory of a life-style free of industrial pursuits (Finney 1975: 181). New Zealand's Maori, although they may have fared better than Hawaii's natives, are also a predominantly urban and proletarianized minority. About 60 per cent of the Maori resided in towns in 1971, a substantial increase from their small 10 per cent population of 1936 (Killick 1976: 69). Although there is an important indigenous cultural movement gaining strength in New Zealand cities, many Maori people cannot speak their ancestral tongue and very few have rights to enough land to make anything but a permanent industrial working life feasible. Noumea, capital of the nickel-producing French Melanesian territory of New Caledonia, is also a European town. Ninety per cent of the Melanesians resident there were working in temporary menial jobs in the early 1960s (Guiart 1963) and seemed blocked in lower positions by the dominant European majority.

If we distinguish between 'less indigenous', 'more indigenous' (cf. McTaggart 1972) and intermediate types of Pacific urbanism, it is clear that Honolulu, Auckland, Wellington and Noumea are representatives of a kind of metropolitan industrial city far removed from nearby and more indigenous Third World centres. With their own territories' indigenes now minority groups, these European industrial centres serve as magnets for labour from the neighbouring islands. Samoan migration to Hawaiian, Californian and New Zealand cities is considerable. Substantial numbers of Tokelauans, Niueans, Tongans and Cook Islanders are found in Auckland and Wellington, New Zealand, as are New Hebrideans, Wallisians and Futumans in Noumea. Although many of these migrants have been shown to maintain or flexibly modify a good deal of their traditional behaviour in their new surroundings through the retention of some extended family ties, chain migration, visiting and strong links to their churches (Ablon 1971, Pitt and McPherson 1974), their overall impact on urban social organization and dominant life-styles is minimal. Well-intentioned New Zealanders, for example, tend to view the 'Islanders' amongst them as a social problem and decry the anomic effects city life has supposedly had upon them. Auckland is certainly not (as it has sometimes been called) 'the world's largest Polynesian city', despite the fact that more Polynesians may live in its decaying inner suburbs than in any other town.

Although these particular South Pacific cities seem to be as unlike the towns in Papua New Guinea as any European centres, it is interesting to note that even in other places (colonized, but not extensively settled by Europeans), urbanization appears to be much less influenced by indigenous socio-cultural practice than in Papua New Guinea. One such area is Tahiti.

Finney (1975) says that Tahitians today are a 'vulnerable proletariate' who have left their traditional life-style of gardening and fishing far behind to take up wage-labour in Papeete, a city which contains two-thirds of French Polynesia's 120,000 people. The urban proletarian-ization of French Polynesia is traced to major investments made in Tahiti's tourist industry and the massive development of the French nuclear testing programme there in the mid-1960s. This case seemingly lends support to theories of urban 'breakdown' so influential in the earlier urban anthropological and sociological literature, as the author stresses the diminution in strength of the extended family, the growth of individualism and the erosion of general reciprocity. Tahitians are quoted making statements indicating the growth of anomie such as 'Formerly we were unified, now it is each man for himself' and 'When it comes to money, one can't trust kinsmen.'

Finney, who has done fieldwork in the Goroka area, feels that a significant difference between Papua New Guinean and Tahitian approaches to urban life is to be found in the latter's lack of an entrepreneurial spirit. While Papua New Guineans think of making investments in rural businesses, Tahitians seem to feel that all they can do is work for others. They see themselves as being too kind to callously profit from their fellows as do Europeans or Chinese businessmen. The few Tahitians who have become entrepreneurs or professionals are called *'apa Popa'a* – 'part European'. The only acceptable niche for 'true Tahitians' is in the working class. Papua New Guineans seem more than willing to fill any urban position they can and, as we have seen, they remain attached to their kinsmen even when upwardly mobile.

It is possible that part of the Tahitian attitude discussed above is due to expatriate dominance of middle- and upper-class positions, and that the putative 'kindness' of Tahitians serves as an ideology to mask this. In any case, French Polynesia is not slated for early independence and the dominant expatriate presence is fundamental to Tahiti's present social structure since the French military and tourist industries are almost the only resources that could sustain a Polynesian urban working class. Papua New Guinea is by contrast a large and potentially rich nation in its own right, which can support towns with a smaller expatriate presence. Fiji, the earliest independent Melanesian nation, also possesses marketable resources in addition to tourism (sugar), but, unlike Papua New Guinea, has a majority Asian population which dominates the country's towns. Urban Fijians (described by Nayacakalou (1963), and Nayacakalou and Southall (1973)) seem to react to urban life in ways which, although similar to Papua New Guineans, nevertheless show the influence of their different cultural background and urban situation.

Although Fijians may be classified as Melanesians, there is a strong Polynesian element discernible in Fiji's indigenous culture. Polynesian societies are characteristically more stratified than those of Melanesia (Sahlins 1963), and Fiji, unlike Papua New Guinea, has hereditary chiefs. This more hierarchical social structure seems conducive to the formation of formal associations in Suva, as Nayacakalou notes that some organizations which engage in important charitable and political activities are run by chiefs. It is interesting, also, that these are built around ties based on place of origin which use district referents. This idiom is similar to that used in Papua New Guinea, although it is differently employed. Another parallel with our case study is found in Fijians' close ties to their villages and urban kin. But unlike most Papua New Guineans, Suva's Fijians develop strong co-operative ties with neighbours from different rural areas, and have thus organized viable unions and other political associations. They also seem to be more committed urbanites, expressing a desire to remain in Suva even after retirement (Nayacakalou 1963: 34–7). We expect that these differences are only partially due to the greater centralization of traditional society in Fiji. The presence of Fijian Indians who dominate business in the country and outnumber Melanesian Fijians in the towns must be a powerful incentive to indigenous organization and solidarity in Fiji as a whole. Indeed, the importation of Indian labour for the sugar fields by the British in colonial times, and the Indians' subsequent domination of the nation's business sector, recalls East Africa more than the rest of the Pacific. Unlike Uganda, however, Melanesian Fijians cannot wish this problem away, as Indo-Fijians make up slightly over 50 per cent of the population.

Not surprisingly, studies from still colonial and more purely Melanesian Island territories show the most compatibility with the Papua New Guinea case. The author of a discussion of urban migrants to Vila and Santo, towns in the New Hebrides, argues that no urban proletariat has formed there because of the importance of one's status as an owner of rural land. Few people call urban centres home (those that do are upwardly mobile) and contact and movement between village and town is regular. The village remains the base from which they participate in a variety of economic activities such as cash-cropping, subsistence gardening, rural business and circular urban migration. This mixed village–urban strategy is seen as a compromise which permits New Hebrideans the option of participating in a new and exciting way of life while maintaining secure traditional ties to the village world (Bedford 1973).

Honiara, capital of the Solomon Islands, seems virtually to be a Papua New Guinean town. Indeed Papua New Guinea itself contains a province, Bougainville, which is historically, geographically and culturally a Solomon Island. These similarities are further reinforced by equivalent colonial experiences as the British (also co-ruler with France of the New Hebrides) seem to have pursued urban policies in their Melanesian colonies which are very similar to those of their Australian counterparts in Papua New Guinea. Melanesians were seen as quintessential rural tribesmen in all three areas and not expected to be more than 'target' urban workers, in town for some fixed period on a temporary basis. With little viable alternative, people remained attached to their villages, intending to return home soon or to retire there eventually. They looked upon the towns as alien places, attractive and exciting, but belonging to the Europeans. Bellam states that Honiara is an almost classic case of the colonial city (1970: 91), but his fieldwork there took place ten years prior to ours in Papua New Guinea. We believe, as we have stressed throughout, that Papua New Guineans have now advanced to the threshold of creating a Melanesian style of urbanism, one which is essentially unique, as most other Melanesian areas are either dominated by non-indigenous immigrants or colonial régimes.

Some overriding similarities

While maintaining that Papua New Guineans are involved in a relatively unique urban situation, we realize that this view is partially a product of having explored a small area in some depth. Although certain important similarities were noted in regions which also have tribal and colonial backgrounds (sub-Saharan Africa and the Island South Pacific), we may have left the impression that the experience of urbanization in Latin America, the Middle East and other areas has few parallels if any with Papua New Guinea. Although the situations in these areas are essentially different, important overriding similarities in world urbanization do exist wherever people from 'backward' rural hinterlands move into modern towns.

Anthropologists and other social scientists who study urbanization in the developing nations have been increasingly impressed by the extent to which urban migrants hold on to their rural customs in the city. Such findings have led to a certain disenchantment with earlier theoretical perspectives on the urbanization process. Louis Wirth's 'Urbanization as a way of life' (1938), which importantly influenced a generation of urban sociologists, had previously postulated a weakening of ties in towns, the decline of the family, the disappearance of neighbourhood solidarity and the loosening of traditional bonds of social cohesion as concomitants of the urbanization process. An essentially similar model was also used by anthropologists. Robert Redfield, who formulated the 'folk–urban continuum' on the basis of a study of Tepoztlan village, Mexico, counterposed the rural and the urban in terms of a contrast between rural homogeneity and solidarity on the one hand, and urban heterogeneity and anonymity on the other. One of the first anthropologists to attack this dichotomy was Oscar Lewis in his well-known restudy of Tepoztlan village and its migrants in Mexico City (1951, 1952). He found that villagers in the metropolis actually modified institutions such as the family, kinship and religion in such a way as to strengthen them in the very urban milieu that was supposed to cause their destruction.

Since then, many urban anthropologists have noted that people migrating to town with few urban relevant skills will use their pre-existing social ties and cultural idioms in an attempt to adapt to urban life. But few social scientists have discussed the effects of this on the development of the towns themselves, which is something we have tried to do in this monograph. We feel that this is necessary to an understanding of the process of urbanization and that, correspondingly, one of the most interesting aspects of the new urban revolution in the developing nations, at least from an anthropological point of view, may well be what McGee (1971: 58) has called the 'ruralization' of the world's cities.

One would expect that towns which experience great and recent migration from the countryside must become substantially affected by this, socially and culturally, be they Latin American, South-East Asian, Indian, Middle Eastern or wherever. Cairo, a huge metropolis inhabited for a thousand years, and as different from Papua New Guinea as any town in the Third World could be, is nevertheless similar to Port Moresby in that the urbanization process is fundamentally affected by rural social idioms in both areas. Egyptians migrating to Cairo also use pre-existing kinship ties to procure initial lodging. Certain Cairenes (particularly Upper Egyptian-born domestic servants) seem to isolate themselves from people other than compatriots while in town, and prefer to live their 'real' lives during visits to the village. Ties to urbanites from the same area are strong as co-villagers tend to be neighbours and spend their off-duty hours socializing in each other's company. Furthermore, Abu-Lughod reports that 'there are vast quarters within the mosaic of Cairo where, physically and socially, the way of life and characteristics of the residents resemble rural Egypt' (1961: 24–5). She notes that, by building a replica of their rural culture and social networks in Cairo, migrants are 'shaping the culture of the city as much as they are adjusting to it' (ibid.: 23).

Thus the dialectical nature of the urbanization process (the fact that migrants are changing the cities at the same time that the cities are changing the migrants) is ubiquitous and provides us with a basic thread of unity in the seemingly bewildering diversity of modern urbanism. Having put the Papua New Guinean experience into comparative perspective, we will, in the following section, summarize the main points made in this monograph.

Summary

The most compelling aspect of Papua New Guinea's towns is the presence of expatriates and indigenous people from all over the country enmeshed in a complex division of labour. The move from small-scale societies, based on subsistence agriculture, organized in terms of kinship idioms and personal forms of leadership, to modern heterogeneous towns characterized by western types of social institutions, ensures that urbanites come into contact with people and situations that have no place in their traditional socio-cultural systems.

But the towns were not alien to Papua New Guineans just because urbanism lay outside their previous experience. The towns that they came to were colonial places under European control, and initially excluded them from any form of meaningful participation in urban life.

The territory was a backwater colony which experienced little real economic development or industrialization in the colonial era: traditional societies remained strong, viable and rural, while small administrative centres grew up in their midst. Variations in contact history, education, and economic development largely set the tone of future differentiation and dispute in the modern state and its towns.

Despite initial exclusion, the increase in administrative spending (most notably in the expansion of education and infrastructure), which was coupled with greater cash-cropping and wage-labour after World War II, led to the growth of an increasingly independent indigenous urban population. This growth in population was not, however, matched by a willingness to acknowledge or provide for the needs of urban migrants. Although skilled natives from coastal areas working for the public service or private firms were gradually provided with good standard housing, many unskilled men either remained poorly housed in barracks or built their own dwellings. These were often erected on vacant government land or, in the case of relatively arid Port Moresby, on land held under native tenure as well. Urban settlements tend to be mono-ethnic or contain ethnic blocs. Most were built far from town centres, or in out-of-the-way places, with few if any services. Indeed, their very existence was either denied or ignored until only a few years ago. Although efforts are currently being made to provide basic services and secure tenure for settlement dwellers in existing areas or new 'no-covenant' ('build-your-own') zones, the housing situation remains critical. The government's present policy, to integrate new housing areas, is an attempt to break down the existing ethnic, racial and social segregation which is a legacy of the indigenous response to the colonial policy of official neglect.

Migrants came to Papua New Guinea's towns for a variety of reasons. Land pressure in densely settled districts, a lack of money-making opportunities, desires for better educational services, an extended adolescence, exciting surroundings, and the chance to get money for rural enterprise, have all been put forward. Regardless of motive, however, migrants are increasingly apt to bring their wives and children to town with them (shifting the urban demography further into line with the rest of the nation), and they are seldom able to save money, especially after the requirements for food, clothing, fellow migrants and rural visitors are met out of the meagre wages of a predominantly unskilled urban population.

The disparities between the pre-war colonial centres and traditional societies were so great that one would have been justified in discussing urbanization and Papua New Guineans in terms of polar opposites. The initial mediating of this opposition (visually apparent in the proliferation of almost hidden, patchy half-tin houses inhabited by poorly dressed, brown-skinned people speaking pidgin languages) had inherent in it a dynamic which has only recently been given room to expand. But it is already apparent that by selectively applying their own social idioms to urban situations Papua New Guineans have begun the transformation of their nation's urban social systems.

New urbanites, whose traditional social milieu is based on rights and obligations defined in kinship terms, attempt to use such pre-existing ties as are available to them in the towns to secure initial housing. From that first night, however, the urban environment makes itself felt in terms of the limited range of kin available to townsmen, their demographic make-up skewed by the migration process, the lack of adequate facilities and the very fact that those resources necessary for urban life are (unlike the village situation) not controlled by kinship groups. Thus even when a migrant is developing a purely personal base of support, his seemingly flexible use of a very basic traditional social idiom is constrained and transformed by the urban environment.

Kinship's importance as an aspect of corporate group membership is diminished in the town and only close kin provide substantial support. A very wide range are, however, approached for small favours or just to pass the time together. In any case, rural kin ties provide for *potential* relationships in town which may be made actual ones by engaging in ongoing urban transactions. Thus urban kinship, based on pre-existing ties, has become a distinctive part of an urban survival strategy. As such, it is used by townsmen to organize their social networks and personal living arrangements. Through the use of such ties, mono-ethnic urban settlements have developed, with overcrowded houses clustered on clan or village lines, and a tendency towards more extended family and multiple nuclear family households. In this way, kinship, itself shaped by the towns, has (via the social forms it produces) left an indelible mark on the urban social landscape.

Because the range of relatives and members of a migrant's rural social group is limited in the town, people often seek to recruit a wider compass of people into their urban social networks. The names of patrol posts, administrative centres, sub-districts and districts (now provinces) provide a terminological scheme for categorizing the variety of people in the towns, and a referent for the development of more inclusive social ties and identities. The flexible (expandable and contractable) nature of this terminological system makes it usable in many social situations. The fact that political conflicts and urban socio-economic differences are associated with the differential provision of rural services and development further reinforces the use of this classificatory scheme, which facilitates the formation of primary ties within relevant, wider than traditional, categories. Cliques of extended kin, to which additional members are recruited by the use of this terminology, become named and perceived as urban ethnic groups by observers and members. Internal differences are played down as even traditional enemies become involved with each other in settlements or at gatherings. Distance from home and urban heterogeneity further diminish the salience of small local differences. The continuing tendency to phrase disputes in group terms and the general need for a wide urban security circle further encourages a wider social orientation.

Townsmen thus adapt their traditional principles of relationship to fit the migration-shaped urban population and cope with the exigencies of the urban environment. The organization of colonial administration and the differential contact and development history create a framework for these urban-based relationships (i.e. an ethnic terminology and set of stereotypes), while specific local events and town–hinterland situations influence the types of interaction and conflict that will occur. Together they fundamentally affect the particular form that urban ethnic agglomerations will take. The more these agglomerations are perceived as ethnic units by outsiders, and labelled as such in various situations, the greater is the tendency for true ethnic groups to emerge in the towns. Thus a social idiom, having distinctly rural referents and channelled by colonial historical factors and particular urban events, has been developed by urban Papua New Guineans. This idiom in turn has become a dominant social theme influencing the entire course of the urbanization process.

The predominance of kinship and ethnicity as principles of urban categorization and association is paralleled by the unimportance of class as a focus of social identity and solidarity. The reluctance to acknowledge an urban hierarchy of occupational prestige as relevant to social relations, the tendency to view low wages and poor conditions as personal issues with specific employers, the lack of substantial industrialization, the instability and fragmentation of the work-force, their unfamiliarity with idioms and methods of industrial relations and their ties to rural people and land, are all aspects of the local situation that contribute to a muting of class consciousness and the accentuation of ethnicity in the wider urban field.

It is possible, however, that class interests will become more engaging in future. Despite the general lack of material on local élites we did note that they seem more class-oriented and more cosmopolitan (in terms of personal friendships) than other urbanites. Similar observations (based on more extensive data and reports) have been made for urban Africa. It has also been suggested that the balance between class and ethnicity in African cities is influenced by 'the size of the highly educated more westernized groups' (Little 1974: 48–9, 95). It is possible that the increasing localization of jobs and the growth of a numerically stronger urban élite will in time give rise to a greater level of class consciousness in Papua New Guinea. Although we would not expect this to result in the eclipse of ethnicity, its great dominance as a factor in urban social action would perhaps be diminished in some social situations. The present policy of integrating housing areas may, if carried further, also have a similar long-term effect.

Although ethnic loyalties may seem to encourage 'provincialism', we have stressed that ethnicity is nevertheless a fundamental component in the development of the *wantok* system, one of the most important elements of the emergent Papua New Guinean urban culture. *Wantok* procedures serve as a mechanism by which the traditional tendency for relations of propinquity to become relations of incorporation, noted for rural areas by Barnes (1962), may be expressed in urban areas. Although the importance of rural corporate groups is diminished in the towns, the *wantok* idiom allows for the recruitment of co-ethnics, work-mates and neighbours to multi-functional personal networks.

Such idioms and principles, developed by Papua New Guineans, are urban social constructions which have begun to transform the very nature of the towns; but their use has not yet been successfully extended nor modified so as to permit the effective integration of local people and the urban bureaucracy. Although certain recreational clubs, church groups and other formal associations have been organized by indigenous townsmen, Papua New Guineans generally have not been successful in developing or dealing with formal organizations.

Although many of the functions that voluntary organizations take on in other countries are handled informally in urban Papua New Guinea, there are limitations to the problems and issues *wantok* groups can cope with. Despite the fact that such links have helped townsmen to deal with the urban bureaucracy, the gap between it and the people remains wide enough to constitute a substantial impediment to the creation of a more integrated Melanesian urban environment.

Future needs: Some problematic aspects of Papua New Guinean urbanization

The future of the ongoing process of creating national urban centres out of former colonial outposts will hinge on the way in which the gap between people and urban institutions is handled. It has been brought out that Papua New Guinean towns, while social systems in their own right, maintain a certain hollowness or lack of integration. The village ideology that has been given so much stress has as its corollary a lack of positive identification with urban centres by their inhabitants. This is manifested in everyday life by an obvious ambivalence to the experience of urban residence on the part of many urbanites. Papua New Guinean townsmen (like the denizens of Honiara, Santo and Vila mentioned in our comparative section) look towards the villages as home and the towns as something still foreign. They are regarded as delightful places, alluring to be sure, but urban life is seen to corrupt and turn people away from more noble responsibilities and actions.

However, the lack of a more positive urban ideology (one which would perhaps help urbanites to overcome the remaining hollowness of their towns) is not merely an epiphenomenon of the strength of rural social systems and the recency of urban migration. To disregard the role of recent colonial policy in excluding natives from towns and doing so little to alleviate the difficulties of the average worker would be as shortsighted as the complacent belief that a Papua New Guinean is and always will be a villager. Such a stance would ignore the progress local people have already made in transforming the urban landscape, and conveniently absolve those in a position of power from their responsibility to correct the policies which have effectively excluded urbanites from the process of decision-making. If the remaining obstacles to further Melanesianization of the urban environment are not removed the present segmented nature of the towns may get worse and their still apparent colonial tinge may deepen rather than fade.

This is most apparent, perhaps, in relation to the towns' emerging social problems. For example, crime, juvenile delinquency and drunkenness are growing at least as fast as the rate of urban population increase, and while they are no more serious than in most other developing areas, these problems are a source of alarm for the local population. They are aggravated by the lack of urban integration and by related feelings of anomie with respect to the wider urban environment. The police, courts and entire Australian-derived justice system are remote from the average urbanite and not accepted as legitimate. The continuing operation of an essentially foreign bureaucracy is seen by many observers as hindering the growth of community in the town as a whole by preventing people from getting together on the local level to solve their problems. Oram (1976) and Clifford (1976) both suggest that 'village courts' and police stations should be set up in urban neighbourhoods and employ people who live there. Their message that the police and justice systems should encourage as much Papua New Guinean participation as possible, both to reduce estrangement from the present apparatus and increase positive identification with its goals, may be extended to other areas. Our previous discussion of the importance of setting up viable city councils as a framework for representing the average citizen in a town-wide, responsive, multi-functional urban institutional framework is another case in point.

If urban institutions are established which give urbanites the opportunity to work together to confront their problems constructively, the legacy of colonial policies, which have produced segregated towns characterized by widespread alienation and hostility between ethnic groups, could be erased. Although specific institutional changes and frameworks will no doubt be subject to continuing debate, the fundamental point, that the bureaucratic gap must be closed for further progressive change to occur, is indisputable.

As was clear from the section on voluntary associations, however, local citizens are not presently in a position to organize themselves for a constructive confrontation with the establishment. Urban institutions will have to be brought to the people in such a way that they can participate in and change them, thus beginning in a new institutional setting, to complete the task of creating a more solid and integrated Papua New Guinean urban environment.

List of references

Ablon, J. 1971. The social organization of an urban Samoan community. *Southwestern Journal of Anthropology*, **27**(2), 75–95.

Abu-Lughod, J. 1961. Migrant adjustment to city life: the Egyptian case. *American Journal of Sociology*, **67**, 22–32.

Allen, B. J. *et al.* 1975. A social survey of Boundary Road settlement, Lae. (Mimeo.) Port Moresby.

Andrews, C. L. 1975. *Business and bureaucracy*. New Guinea Research Bulletin no. 59. Port Moresby and Canberra: New Guinea Research Unit and Australian National University.

Ballard, J. 1976. *Wantoks and administration*. Public lecture. (Mimeo.) Port Moresby: University of Papua New Guinea.

Banton, M. 1973. Urbanisation and role theory. In *Urban anthropology: cross-cultural studies of urbanisation*, ed. A. Southall, pp. 43–70. London: Oxford University Press.

Barnes, J. A. 1962. African models in the New Guinea Highlands. *Man*, **62**, 5–9.

Barth, F. 1966. *Models of social organisation*. Occasional Paper. London: Royal Anthropological Institute.

1971. Tribes and inter-tribal relations in the Fly headwaters. *Oceania*, **41**, 171–91.

Bates, R. 1973. *Ethnicity in contemporary Africa*. Eastern African Studies no. 14. Syracuse: Syracuse University.

Bateson, G. 1936. *Naven*. Palo Alto: Stanford University Press.

Baxter, M. W. P. 1973. *Migration and the Orokaiva*. Dept. of Geography Occasional Paper no. 3. Port Moresby: University of Papua New Guinea.

Bedford, R.D. 1973. *New Hebridean mobility: a study of circular migration*. Canberra: Australian National University.

Bedford, R. D. and A. Mamak. 1976. Bougainvilleans in urban wage employment: some aspects of migrant flows and adaptive strategies. *Oceania*, **46**(3), 169–87.

Bell, D. 1975. Ethnicity and social change. In *Ethnicity theory and experience*, eds. N. Glazer and D. P. Moynihan, pp. 141–76. Cambridge, Mass.: M.I.T. Press.

Bell, H. 1967. Goodbye to all that?: integration in the PIR. *New Guinea*, **2**(2), 49–58.

Bellam, M. E. P. 1970. The colonial city: Honiara, a Pacific Islands case study. *Pacific Viewpoint*, **2**(1), 66–96.

Belshaw, C. S. 1957. *The great village: the economic and social welfare of Hanuabada, an urban community in Papua*. London: Routledge and Kegan Paul.

Bendix, R. and S. M. Lipset. 1967. Karl Marx's theory of social classes. In *Class, status and power*, eds. R. Bendix and S. M. Lipset, pp. 6–11. New York: Free Press.

Berger, P. and T. Luckmann. 1966. *The social construction of reality*. New York: Doubleday.

Biksup, P., B. Jinks and H. Nelson. 1968. *A short history of New Guinea.* Sydney: Angus and Robertson.

Blumer, H. 1969. *Symbolic interactionism.* Englewood Cliffs, New Jersey: Prentice-Hall.

Breese, G. 1966. *Urbanisation in newly developing countries.* Englewood Cliffs, New Jersey: Prentice-Hall.

Brookfield, H. C. 1960. Population distribution and labour migration in New Guinea: a preliminary survey. *Australian Geographer,* 7, 233–42.

Brookfield, H. C. with D. Hart. 1971. *Melanesia: a geographical interpretation of an island world.* London: Methuen.

Brown, P. 1970. Chimbu transactions. *Man,* 5, 99–117.

Bruner, E. M. 1963. Medan: the role of kinship in an Indonesian city. In *Pacific port towns and cities,* ed. A. Spoehr, pp. 1–12. Honolulu: Bishop Museum Press.

Bulmer, S. 1975. Settlement and economy in prehistoric Papua New Guinea: a review of the archeological evidence. *Oceanistes,* 31, 7–75.

Chowning, A., T. S. Epstein, J. Goodale and I. Grosart. 1971. Under the volcano. In *The politics of dependence, Papua New Guinea 1968,* eds. A. L. Epstein *et al.,* pp. 48–90. Canberra: Australian National University Press.

Clifford, W. 1976. Crime prevention in Papua New Guinea. In *Crime in Papua New Guinea,* ed. D. Biles, pp. 79–90. Canberra: Australian Institute of Criminology.

Colebatch, H. K., P. Colebatch, M. Reay and A. J. Strathern. 1971. Free elections in a guided democracy. In *The politics of dependence, Papua New Guinea 1968,* eds. A. L. Epstein *et al.,* pp. 218–74. Canberra: Australian National University Press.

Conroy, J. D. 1972. Urbanisation: a development constraint. *Economic Record,* 46, 497–516.

1973. *Occupational prestige, economic rationality and labour market behaviour in Papua New Guinea.* Dept. of Economics Discussion Paper. Port Moresby: University of Papua New Guinea.

Conroy, J. D. and R. Curtain. 1973. Migrants in an urban economy: rural school leavers in Port Moresby. *Oceania,* 44, 81–95.

Crocombe, R. 1969. The debate goes on. *New Guinea,* 4(3), 49–58.

Curtain, R. 1975. Labour migration in Papua New Guinea: primary school leavers in the towns – present and future significance. In *Migration and development,* eds. H. I. Safa and B. M. DuToit, pp. 269–93. The Hague: Mouton.

Das Gupta, J. 1975. Ethnicity, language demands and national development in India. In *Ethnicity, theory and experience,* eds. N. Glazer and D. P. Moynihan, pp. 466–88. Cambridge, Mass.: Harvard University Press.

Department of Geography, University of Papua New Guinea. 1974. *Report to the Housing Commission on a socio-economic survey of Ranuguri settlement, Port Moresby.* (Mimeo.) Port Moresby: University of Papua New Guinea.

Department of Labour, Papua New Guinea. 1969. *Report on the Highlands labour scheme.* Port Moresby: National Archives.

Doughty, P. L. 1970. Behind the back of the city: 'provincial' life in Lima, Peru. In *Peasants in cities: readings in the anthropology of urbanisation,* ed. W. Mangin, pp. 30–46. Boston: Houghton Mifflin.

Encyclopedia of Papua and New Guinea. 1972. General ed. P. Ryan. Melbourne:

Melbourne University Press in association with the University of Papua New Guinea.

Epstein, A. L. 1958. *Politics in an urban African community.* Manchester: Manchester University Press.

1967. Occupational prestige on the Gazelle Peninsula, New Britain. *Australian and New Zealand Journal of Sociology*, 3, 111–21.

1969. *Matupit: land, politics and change among the Tolai of New Britain.* Berkeley: University of California Press.

1970. Aspects of political development on the Gazelle Peninsula. In *The politics of Melanesia*, Fourth Waigani Seminar, ed. M. W. Ward, pp. 105–22. Port Moresby: University of Papua New Guinea.

Ethnographic Bibliography of New Guinea. 1968. 3 vols. Department of Anthropology and Sociology, Australian National University. Canberra: Australian National University Press.

Fallers, L. A. 1967. *Immigrants and associations.* The Hague: Mouton and Co.

Ferraro, G. P. 1973. Tradition or transition, rural and urban kinsmen in East Africa. *Urban Anthropology*, 2(2), 214–31.

Finney, B. R. 1975. A vulnerable proletariat: Tahitians in the 1970s. In *The impact of urban centers in the Pacific*, eds. R. Force and B. Bishop, pp. 181–92. Honolulu: Pacific Science Association.

Fitzpatrick, P. and L. Blaxter. 1976. Legislating urbanism. In *An introduction to the urban geography of Papua New Guinea*, ed. R. T. Jackson, pp. 79–87. Dept. of Geography Occasional Paper no. 13. Port Moresby: University of Papua New Guinea.

Garnaut, R. Forthcoming. Urban growth: an interpretation of trends and choices. In *Change and movement, readings on internal migration in Papua New Guinea*, ed. R. J. May. Canberra: Australian National Press.

Geertz, C. 1963. The integrative revolution: primordial sentiments and civil politics in the new states. In *Old societies and new states*, ed. C. Geertz, pp. 105–57. New York: Free Press.

Grillo, R. D. 1974. Ethnic identity and social stratification on a Kampala housing estate. In *Urban ethnicity*, A. S. A. Monograph no. 12, ed. A. Cohen, pp. 159–86. London: Tavistock.

Gugler, J. 1975. Migration and ethnicity in sub-Saharan Africa: affinity, rural interests and urban alignments. In *Migration and development*, eds. H. I. Safa and B. M. DuToit, pp. 295–310. The Hague: Mouton.

Guiart, J. 1963. Noumea, New Caledonia. In *Pacific port towns and cities: a symposium*, ed. A. Spoehr. Honolulu: Bishop Museum Press.

Gulick, J. 1974. Urban anthropology. In *Handbook of social and cultural anthropology*, ed. J. J. Honigmann, pp. 979–1029. Chicago: Rand McNally.

Gutkind, P. C. W. 1974. *Urban anthropology: perspectives on third world urbanisation and urbanism.* Assen: Van Gorcum.

Hanna, W. J. and J. L. Hanna. 1971. *Urban dynamics in black Africa.* Chicago: Aldine Atherton.

Harding, T. G. 1967. *Voyagers of the Vitiaz Strait: a study of a New Guinea trade system.* Seattle: University of Washington Press.

1971. Wage labour and cash cropping: the economic adaptation of New Guinea copra producers. *Oceania*, 41, 192–200.

Harries-Jones, P. 1969. 'Home-Boy' ties and political organization in a copperbelt township. In *Social networks in urban situations*, ed. J. C. Mitchell, pp. 297–347. Manchester: Manchester University Press.

Harris, G. T. 1972. Internal migration in Papua New Guinea: a survey of recent literature. Unpublished paper. Port Moresby: University of Papua New Guinea.

1974. Internal migration in Papua New Guinea: a survey of recent literature. *Yagl-Ambu*, 1(2).

Hitchcock, N. and N. D. Oram (eds.) 1967. *Rabia Camp: a Port Moresby migrant settlement*. New Guinea Research Bulletin no. 14. Port Moresby and Canberra: Australian National University.

Jackson, R. T. 1976a. (ed.) *An introduction to the urban geography of Papua New Guinea*. Dept. of Geography Occasional Paper no. 13. Port Moresby: University of Papua New Guinea.

1976b. A social geography of urban Papua New Guinea. In *An introduction to the urban geography of Papua New Guinea*, ed. R. T. Jackson, pp. 28–70. Dept. of Geography Occasional Paper no. 13. Port Moresby: University of Papua New Guinea.

1977. The growth, nature and future prospects of informal settlements in Papua New Guinea. *Pacific Viewpoint*, 18(1), 22–42.

Jackson, R. T. and D. K. Forbes. 1975. *A social survey of Nuigo, Wewak*. (Mimeo.) Port Moresby.

Joyce, R. 1971. *Sir William MacGregor*. Melbourne: Oxford University Press.

Kapferer, B. (ed.) 1976. *Transaction and meaning*. Philadelphia: Institute for the Study of Human Issues.

Killick, N. G. (ed.) 1976. *New Zealand Official Yearbook*. Wellington: Government Printer.

Lea, D. and H. Weinand. 1971. Some consequences of population growth in the Wosera Area East Sepik District. In *Population growth and socio-economic change*. New Guinea Research Unit Bulletin no. 42, pp. 122–36. Canberra: Australian National University Press.

Levine, H. B. 1976. The formation of ethnic units in urban Papua New Guinea. Unpublished. Ph.D. dissertation, State University of New York at Stony Brook. Ann Arbor: University Microfilms.

1977. Comment on 'Family, fertility and economics' by W. P. Handwerker. *Current Anthropology*, 18(2), 270.

Lewis, O. 1951. *Life in a Mexican village: Tepoztlan restudied*. Urbana: University of Illinois Press.

1952. Urbanization without breakdown. *Scientific Monthly*, 75, 31–41.

Little, K. 1957. The role of voluntary associations in West African urbanization. *American Anthropologist*, 59, 579–96.

1973. *African women in towns*. Cambridge: Cambridge University Press.

1974. *Urbanization as a social process*. London: Routledge and Kegan Paul.

Lloyd, P. C. 1974. *Power and independence: urban Africans' perception of social inequality*. London: Routledge and Kegan Paul.

Lucas, J. 1972. Lae – a town in transition. *Oceania*, 42(4), 260–75.

McGee, T. G. 1971. *The urbanization process in the third world*. London: G. Bell and Son.

McTaggart, W. D. 1972. Urbanization in the South Pacific and the case of Noumea. In *Man in the Pacific Islands*, ed. R. G. Ward, pp. 280–328. Oxford: Clarendon Press.

Mair, L. P. 1970. *Australia in New Guinea*. Melbourne: Melbourne University Press.

154   *Urbanization in Papua New Guinea*

Malinowski, B. 1922. *Argonauts of the Western Pacific*. London: Routledge and Kegan Paul.
Mamak, A. and R. Bedford. 1974. Bougainville's students. *New Guinea*, 9(1), 4–15.
Martin, R. M. 1969. Tribesmen into trade unionists: the African experience and the Papua New Guinea prospect. *Journal of Industrial Relations*, 2(2), 125–72.
May, R. J. and R. Skelton. 1975. *Internal migration in Papua New Guinea: an introduction to its description and analysis*. Discussion Paper no. 4. Port Moresby: New Guinea Research Unit.
Mayer, P. 1961. *Townsmen or tribesmen*. Cape Town: Oxford University Press.
Metcalfe, P. A. 1968. Port Moresby's Papuan workers and their association. Unpublished M.A. thesis, University of Auckland.
Mihalic, F. 1971. *The Jacaranda dictionary and grammar of Melanesian pidgin*. Marrickville: Jacaranda Press.
Mitchell, J. C. 1956. *The Kalela dance*. The Rhodes-Livingstone Papers no. 27. Manchester: Manchester University Press.
    1966. Theoretical orientations in African urban studies. In *The social anthropology of complex societies*, A. S. A. Monograph no. 4, ed. M. Banton, pp. 37–68. London: Tavistock.
Munster, P. M. 1973. The ground of the ancestors, Part I: a history of Goroka. Unpublished M.A. thesis, University of Papua New Guinea.
Nayacakalou, R. R. 1963. The urban Fijians of Suva. In *Pacific port towns and cities*, ed. A. Spoehr. Honolulu: Bishop Museum Press.
Nayacakalou, R. R. and A. Southall. 1973. Urbanization and Fijian cultural traditions in the context of Pacific port cities. In *Urban anthropology: cross-cultural studies of urbanization*, ed. A. Southall, pp. 393–405. New York: Oxford University Press.
Oeser, L. 1969. *Hohola: the significance of social networks in the urban adaptation of women in Papua New Guinea's first low cost housing estate*. New Guinea Research Unit Bulletin no. 29. Canberra: Australian National University.
O'Neill, R. J. 1971. The army in Papua New Guinea. *New Guinea*, 6 6–27.
Oram, N. D. 1967. Rabia Camp and the Tommy Kabu Movement. In *Rabia Camp: a Port Moresby migrant settlement*, eds. N. Hitchcock and N. D. Oram. New Guinea Research Unit Bulletin no. 14. Canberra: Australian National University.
    1968. The Hula in Port Moresby. *Oceania*, 39(4), 243–75.
    1970. Indigenous housing in Port Moresby. In *Port Moresby urban development*, eds. J. V. Langmore and N. D. Oram, pp. 45–88. New Guinea Research Unit Bulletin no. 37. Canberra: Australian National University.
    1972. Urban administration. In *Encyclopedia of Papua and New Guinea*, gen. ed. P. Ryan, pp. 1156–62. Melbourne: Melbourne University Press in association with the University of Papua New Guinea.
    1976. *Colonial town to Melanesian city*. Canberra: Australian National University Press.
Papua New Guinea Census. 1971. *Papua New Guinea Census Reports*. Port Moresby: Government Printer.
Papua New Guinea Newsletter. 21 January 1977. Port Moresby: Office of Information.
Parratt, J. K. 1971. Religious change in Port Moresby. *Oceania*, 41, 106–13.

Pitt, D. and C. McPherson. 1974. *Emerging pluralism: the Samoan community in New Zealand*. Auckland: Longman Paul.

Plotnicov, L. 1970. Nigerians: the dream is unfulfilled. In *Peasants in cities*, ed. W. Mangin, pp. 170–4. Boston: Houghton Mifflin.

Ranson, B. 1972. The cop and the beat. *New Guinea*, **7**, 36–42.

Rew, A. 1974. *Social images and process in urban New Guinea; a study of Port Moresby*. St Paul: West Publishing Company.

Rollwagen, J. R. 1975. Introduction: the city as context: a symposium. *Urban Anthropology*, **3**, 1–4.

Rowley, C. D. 1958. *The Australians in German New Guinea*. Melbourne: Melbourne University Press.

Ryan, D. 1968. The migrants. *New Guinea*, **2**, 60–6.

1970. Rural and urban villagers; a bi-local social system in Papua. Unpublished Ph.D. thesis, University of Hawaii.

Sack, P. G. 1973. *Land between two laws; early European land aquisitions in New Guinea*. Canberra: Australian National University Press.

Sahlins, M. 1963. Poor man, rich man, big man, chief: political types in Melanesia and Polynesia. *Comparative Studies in Society and History*, **5**, 285–303.

1965. On the sociology of primitive exchange. In *The relevance of models for social anthropology*, A. S. A. Monograph no. 1, ed. M. Banton, pp. 139–236. London: Tavistock.

Salisbury, M. E. and R. F. Salisbury. 1970. Siane migrant workers in Port Moresby. *Industrial Review (Papua New Guinea)*, **8**(2), 5–11.

1972. The rural oriented strategy of urban adaptation: Siane migrants in Port Moresby. In *The anthropology of urban environments*, Monograph no. 11, eds. T. Weaver and D. White, pp. 49–68. Washington, D.C.: Society for Applied Anthropology.

Salisbury, R. F. 1967. Highland workers in Port Moresby. Unpublished paper. Port Moresby: University of Papua New Guinea.

Seifert, W. 1975. Adjustment to urbanisation in Papua New Guinea. Unpublished Ph.D. dissertation, Catholic University of America, Washington, D.C.

Simic, A. 1973. *The peasant urbanites, a study of rural–urban mobility in Serbia*. New York: Seminar Press.

Somare, M. 1975. *Sana, an autobiography of Michael Somare*. Port Moresby: Niugini Press.

Southall, A. 1973a. Introduction. In *Urban anthropology: cross-cultural studies of urbanization*, ed. A. Southall, pp. 3–14. London: Oxford University Press.

1973b. The density of role-relationships as a universal index of urbanization. In *Urban anthropology: cross-cultural studies of urbanization*, ed. A. Southall, pp. 71–106. London: Oxford University Press.

Stevenson, M. 1968. A trade union in New Guinea. *Oceania*, **39**, 110–36.

Strathern, A. J. 1971. *The rope of moka: big-men and ceremonial exchange in Mount Hagen, New Guinea*. Cambridge: Cambridge University Press.

1974. When dispute procedures fail. In *Contention and dispute: aspects of law and social control in Melanesia*, ed. A. L. Epstein, pp. 240–70. Canberra: Australian National University Press.

1976. Seven good men: the Dei open electorate. In *Prelude to self-government*, ed. D. Stone, pp. 265–84. Canberra: Research School of Pacific Studies and University of Papua New Guinea at Australian National University.

Strathern, M. 1972. Absentee businessmen: the reaction at home to Hageners migrating to Port Moresby. *Oceania*, **43**, 19–39.

1975. *No money on our skins: Hagen migrants in Port Moresby*. New Guinea Research Bulletin no. 61. Port Moresby and Canberra: Australian National University.

Forthcoming. The disconcerting tie: attitudes of Hagen migrants towards home. In *Internal migration in Papua New Guinea*, ed. R. J. May, Canberra: Australian National University Press.

Stuart, I. 1970. *Port Moresby: yesterday and today*. Sydney: Pacific Publications.

Surmon, A. V. 1971. The residential pattern of a colonial town, Port Moresby. Unpublished M.A. thesis, University of Papua New Guinea.

Tufman, M. Z. 1974. The role of police in Papua New Guinea. *Australia and New Zealand Journal of Criminology*, **7**, 87–94.

Ward, R. G. 1971. Internal migration and urbanisation in Papua New Guinea. In *Population growth and socio-economic change*. New Guinea Research Unit Bulletin no. 42, pp. 81–107. Port Moresby and Canberra: Australian National University.

Weber, M. 1961. Ethnic groups. In *Theories of society*, eds. T. Parsons, E. Shils, K. Naegele and J. Pitts, vol. 1, pp. 305–9. New York: Free Press.

1966. The development of caste. In *Class status and power*, 2nd edn, eds. R. Bendix and S. M. Lipset, pp. 28–36. New York: Free Press.

West, F. J. 1956. Colonial development in central New Guinea. *Pacific Affairs*, **29**, 161–73.

1968. *Hubert Murray*. Melbourne: Melbourne University Press.

Whiteman, J. 1973. *Chimbu family relationships in Port Moresby*. New Guinea Research Unit Bulletin no. 52. Port Moresby and Canberra: Australian National University.

Willis, I. 1974. *Lae, village and city*. Melbourne: Melbourne University Press.

Wirth, L. 1938. Urbanisation as a way of life. *American Journal of Sociology*, **54**, 1–24.

Wolfers, E. P. 1976. Towards self-government. The perspective of 1971. In *Prelude to self-government*, ed. D. Stone, pp. 1–24. Canberra: Research School of Pacific Studies and University of Papua New Guinea at Australian National University.

Wright, M. 1975. *Towards an understanding of being without formal employment in Papua New Guinea towns*. Discussion Paper no. 9. Port Moresby: New Guinea Research Unit.

Zimmerman, L. 1973. Migration and urbanisation among the Buang of Papua New Guinea. Unpublished Ph.D. thesis, Wayne State University, Michigan.

Index